Contents

To start you off

This book is called *The People Who Came* because it tells how people came to our part of the world, and what their life was like. You will learn about the earliest Americans, the Indians who were here for thousands of years before Columbus came; you will learn, too, about the people who came after Columbus – the Africans, the Indians from the east, the Chinese and the Europeans. All of us who now live in the Americas are the descendants of immigrants to this part of the world, even though many of these people came here thousands of years ago.

This book will tell you something of how the Indians lived in America before the Europeans came. It will also tell you about the life of the later immigrants to the New World before they left their homelands. But the book will also give you things to think about. If, in reading, you use your imagination and your mind, as well as your eyes, you will discover an interesting fact: people are very much alike all over the world. In every country they provide themselves with food and shelter. They worship. They express their ideas of beauty in painting, crafts, building or music. They learn to live together. They develop their own kind of civilisation.

At the end of each chapter there are suggestions of things for you to do. Before you begin, provide yourself with a scrapbook and divide the scrapbook into sections, one for each chapter. At the beginning of each section of your scrapbook draw an outline map of the region you will be reading about and, when you have finished the chapter, mark on the map all the places mentioned. Write in your scrapbook the answers to the questions, and put in it any of the drawings you are asked to make. If you read any of the suggested books, write book reviews and add them to your scrapbook. Do not neglect to look in newspapers and magazines for any pictures of the places you read about. These, too, go into the scrapbook. Finally, at the end of each section, make a glossary of any new words you learnt in the chapter, especially foreign words. If you keep your scrapbook carefully you will have an attractive record of your own work to show at home and to keep as you go up the school.

You can learn a great deal about the earliest Americans by looking at good pictures. Look in your local Public Library to see if they have any books on the early Americans.

I hope you will very much enjoy learning about *the people who came*.

Alma Norman

PART ONE

THE FIRST TO COME

CHAPTER ONE

'Man travels the road of history'

Scientists think that the earliest men on earth may have lived about 3 million years ago. We would not have recognised them as men, however, for their posture was stooped and their bodies were covered with hair. Their foreheads were low and sloping, and they had jaws which jutted out in front of their noses.

During hundreds of thousands of years these very early men slowly developed an upright posture. They became less hairy, and their brains grew larger. By about 50,000 B.C. they looked very much like ourselves. We give these modern-looking men the name *Homo Sapiens*, which is the name by which the human race is known today. Some time during this long period when cave-men were developing into Homo Sapiens, the division of mankind into different races took

Man: the first tool-making animal in the world. The earliest recorded man-made tools are stone tools made in Ethiopia in Africa over 2 million years ago!

place. Men became Negroid (the black race), Caucasoid (the white race) or Mongoloid (the yellow race).

Our information from early, or pre-historic man, comes from *archaeology*. An archaeologist is someone who finds out about the past by studying the remains of buildings and *artefacts* (tools and utensils made by man) which people have left behind. Often these artefacts are found in graves, so that archaeologists are often able to tell something about the size and build of the people of the past, as well as their customs. Ancient people buried all sorts of things with their dead, including ornaments and pottery. In addition to finding these things, archaeologists have also discovered paintings made by these people on the walls of caves, and these too tell us a good deal about how they lived. Some of these wall paintings are shown on page 4. Notice how each painting tells a story.

Archaeologists use several methods to discover how old artefacts are. They can often make quite an accurate guess by seeing how deep in the ground the artefacts are. Obviously, the closer the objects are to the surface the less old they will be.

Sometimes, archaeologists find objects which provide good clues about their age. For example, coins are very useful because they generally show the year in which they were made. If a coin is found amongst a lot of other artefacts we can guess that all the artefacts are about as old as the coin is. Can you think of other objects which provide good clues to archaeologists?

However, for very old objects which come from such a long time ago that we have no clue about their age archaeologists have to use a special scientific method which involves a complicated chemical analysis of the artefact. This test, which is called the *Carbon-14* test, enables the archaeologist to date very accurately artefacts which are hundreds of thousands of years old! In this way the archaeologist is able to tell us how long ago cave men learned to use fire and when they began to cultivate their own food instead of hunting animals and gathering wild fruit.

The beginning of human progress

Food cultivation, or agriculture, is the beginning of all human progress. Let us see why this is so. When men are hunters they cannot settle in one place. They must follow the animals for food. But once man began to plant seeds, he found he had to wait on them to mature, and so he settled in one place. Soon he began to erect permanent buildings. The population increased, because the supply of food was sure. Eventually it was found that a few farmers could feed many people, so that people began to specialise and develop many different skills. The roving hunters became a settled community.

In this settled community, some people became tool-makers, some potters, others weavers. Those who farmed developed the art of irrigation: how to use canals to bring water to their crops. They also studied the movements of the moon, the planets and the stars, because they felt that there was a connection between these bodies and the weather. Their crops might also grow better when the stars were in certain positions. Gradually a group emerged who devoted all their time to the study of the heavens, and the farmers came to depend upon the accuracy of their observations for the success of their agriculture. Out of these observations the first calendars were invented. Using the calendars, it became possible to foretell the movements of the stars, moon and the sun.

But because the ordinary people did not know the reasons behind the movement of the stars and planets, they came to feel that those who foretold their movements possessed special gifts, and were perhaps favoured by the gods. It is easy to understand, therefore, why many of those who seemed to have special knowledge of the heavens became the priests or religious leaders of the community. Others, with different talents, became the artists of the tribe. Some became inventors, like the one who discovered the wheel, or the first person to find out that putting clay in the fire produced a superior pot.

The community also had to be governed, and so a leader emerged, who made laws and enforced them. As the community grew stronger and wealthier, it produced more goods than it needed, and it began to trade with other communities. As people traded they exchanged ideas as well as goods, and so increased their knowledge in many ways. Yet none of this would have been possible without agriculture. We see, therefore, that agriculture is the foundation on which all civilisation is built.

Let us stop here for a moment and imagine the history of man as a vast rolling countryside. There are many hills in the countryside, and a few towering peaks. These peaks represent the great achievements which man has made, and his great strides forward. In this book we shall learn about some of these, especially those that have contributed in some way to the development of our West Indian community.

Three stages in the development of man.

3

A hunting scene.

A battle scene. Notice that one warrior is holding a weapon rather like a boomerang.

Thousands of years ago the Sahara was not a dry desert area. It had sufficient water to support river animals, as this picture of a crocodile shows.

The three pictures on this page are copies of wall paintings found in the Sahara Desert. They are believed to have been made about 8,000 years ago.

CHAPTER TWO

Coming to the Americas

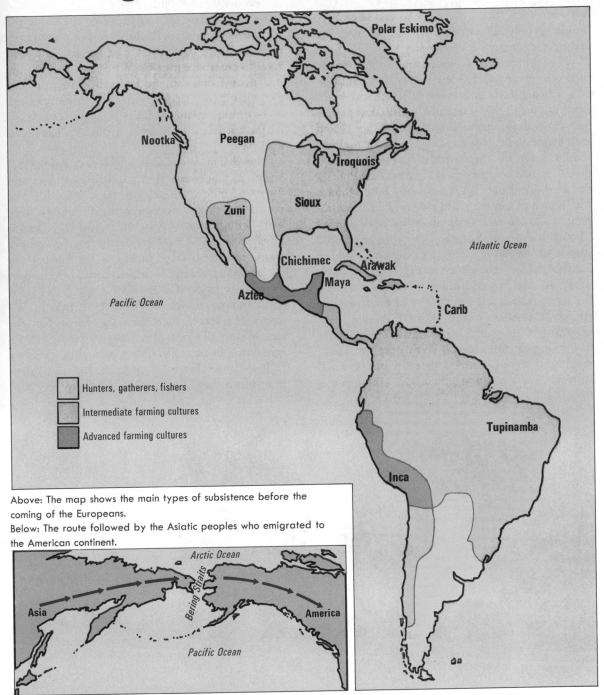

Above: The map shows the main types of subsistence before the coming of the Europeans.
Below: The route followed by the Asiatic peoples who emigrated to the American continent.

We who live in the Caribbean might be called 'people on the move'. Our people have always migrated from the Caribbean to other regions. In the past, people also migrated in great numbers *to* the Caribbean. They came from Africa, from Asia, and from Europe. When they arrived, however, they found people who had been here thousands of years before them. These were the early Americans.

When the Spaniards came to the Americas in the fifteenth century there were nearly thirty million people living on the continents of North and South America, and the West Indian islands. These people lived in widely separated settlements. Some had their homes in the bleak and barren Arctic regions; some lived in the forests and around the lakes of eastern Canada, while others inhabited the Prairies or Great Plains of what is now the United States. Much further south, in what we now call Central America, there were settlements in the Valley of Mexico and on the Yucatan Peninsula, and in the islands of the West Indies. On the continent of South America people were living in certain parts of the Amazonian rainforests of the east, and on the west coast deserts, as well as in the towering Andes Mountains. Some of these people were very simple but others were highly civilised and had built great cities and powerful empires. There were hunters and farmers, warriors and, as in all cultures, builders among the early Americans.

The first settlers in the Americas

As we read in Chapter 1, man may have appeared on the earth about 3 million years ago. The first men in the Americas seem to have appeared between fifteen thousand and twenty thousand years ago, during the fourth Ice Age. During the Ice Ages large parts of the earth were covered with ice, and much of the water of oceans, lakes and rivers were frozen into ice. We do not really know *how* people first came to be in the Americas, but there is a theory that they came to America from Asia during the fourth Ice Age. If we look at the map we will be able to see how this may have been possible.

The *Bering Straits* are only ninety kilometres wide, and between the mainlands of Asia and North America there are three islands. The maximum distance between these islands is only forty kilometres so that on a clear day land is always visible. Moreover, the Bering Sea is only 40 metres deep, so that during the Ice Age parts of it could have frozen enough to form a land bridge. We can understand, then, how it was possible for wanderers to cross the straits to the Americas. We say wanderers rather than migrants, for the newcomers did not plan to set up new homes when they came. Most likely, being hunters, they followed the herds of animals like the giant mammoth, and continued to follow the herd

The Giant Mammoth.

without knowing that they were in a new land.

During these millennia (thousands of years), the newcomers travelled in many directions. There were ice-free corridors many kilometres wide, especially in the west, so that the people were able to find their way into the interior of America. Eventually some of them wandered southward until they reached *Mexico* and the *Isthmus of Panama*, and some of them continued even further southward into South America. It is also likely that some people reached South America from islands in the Pacific Ocean. We don't know how these people managed to travel such great distances, nor how they overcame the many obstacles, but we know that they were the ancestors of many of the Indians of the Americas.

How early man developed

Trying to find out *how* man lived is more difficult than finding out *when* he lived. It's like working out an exciting jigsaw puzzle: you find one piece of evidence, and then another, and yet another, and when you have put all the pieces together you have a picture of how they developed.

We know from how other prehistoric men were living in other parts of the world at the same time, that the Indians of the Americas already possessed some skills when they came. They could make fire; they could make tools of stone and bone; they knew how to hunt large animals by digging pits into which they stampeded them, and they knew how to catch small game by the use of snares. They had brought dogs with them from Asia, and they used them as beasts of burden. Using stone knives and scrapers they skinned the animals they killed and used the skins for clothing.

Like all peoples, the American Indians also learnt eventually to use plants as a source of food. First they used only wild seeds, but they finally learnt to cultivate these seeds, and thus became farmers who depended upon agriculture.

The American Indians began to develop into farmers about nine thousand years ago. Farming developed in all parts of the Americas. Root crops like yam and cassava and potato developed in the tropical regions of the Caribbean and South America, while seed crops developed in the Mexican highlands. The most important of all these crops was the seed crop, corn, especially the variety called *zea mays* from which our present-day sweet corn has developed. The great importance of corn is that it does not seed itself but must be cultivated. This means that the people who came to depend upon corn for their subsistence had to settle in one place and tend the crop for a long time.

As we read in Chapter 1, once people begin to depend upon agriculture rather than on hunting for their food supply, they can grow a surplus of food and thus support a larger population. Furthermore, not everyone, in this situation, needs to farm. Some are able to develop other skills. This is because, unlike hunters, farming groups have time (or leisure) between crops, to develop crafts and better building techniques. It becomes possible to develop what we call a civilisation. We shall see as we read further in this book that it was those who produced a surplus of food who also developed the great Indian civilisations of the Americas.

There were other skills, too, which the Indians were learning over the centuries. They learnt to make pottery, and eventually to make fire-hardened pots. This was done by putting the dried

What an early North American Indian family might have looked like.

7

The colour schemes of early Peruvian textiles were brilliant, using a wide range of dyes. This example, found in an ancient grave, is the work of a master-weaver.

clay in a hot fire and leaving it there for sever days until all the moisture had disappeared. In th way the clay became very hard and the pots wer not so likely to break. Making fire-hardened po represented a great technical advance. Often the pots were also beautifully decorated and painted The Indians learnt also to cultivate cotton and t weave fine cloth.

As they had more leisure, and developed mor technical skills, they also learnt to use metal t make ornaments of gold and silver, and to mak some tools of copper and bronze. Their artists an craftsmen developed the arts of painting and c sculpturing in stone. Eventually, as we shall se some of them developed the arts of architecture even without the widespread use of metal tools Not all the Indians developed in these ways o course. Some remained hunters, or practised subsistence agriculture. This means that they pro duced enough food to survive but not enough t produce a surplus. Such groups could not and di not develop the interest, nor the technology, fo building in the grand style. Instead of great ston cities, they built simple buildings, using wha readily available material they found near at hand

The Indians of the Americas did not onl develop different ways of living. Over the cen turies they also developed variations in appear ance. All of them were brown-skinned, witl straight black hair, but some were a dark copper brown, while others had a paler colouring, like the Eskimo. Some were tall and had stright noses and thin lips, like the Indians of North America Others, like the Indians of Mexico, Central and South America and the West Indies, were shorter. with full mouths and rather flat noses. The Eskimo looked more like these southern people than like the North American Indians.

In Amerindian Societies, as in most other societies at that time of history including Europe, society was much more closely knit than is the case today. Home and work were not so completely separated. Men, women and children all had important, though different, roles to play in providing food, clothing and shelter for the family, and in assuming responsibilities towards the community as a whole.

In most Amerindian societies the role of the

woman was essential for the production and marketing of agricultural produce, as well as the making of clothing and of the various types of baskets used as household utensils. As might be expected women were also responsible for the care and raising of children, though boys in many societies were removed from their mother's care at an early age so that they could be trained by the men for the responsibilities of manhood. Despite women's great importance, however, they were not treated as equals. Although in some Amerindian societies – for instance amongst the Aztec – women had certain legal rights, in other societies – such as the Carib – this seems not to have been the case.

Undoubtedly, also, there were in all societies women of outstanding intelligence and talent who had more power and influence than was usual for women. Such, for example, were the 'Chosen Women' among the Inca, about whom you will read. It is possible, too, that in all societies decisions made by the men who ruled were sometimes influenced by the wise and practical suggestions of wives or mothers.

Over thousands of years the Indians who came to America slowly built up their own way of life. When the Spaniards came to our part of the world in the fifteenth century they called it the *New World*. But to the Indians of the Americas, as we have seen, it was already very old.

Things to do and think about

1 Use a physical map of the Americas and find out what physical features would have helped the early Americans to travel. Which would have hindered them? Draw an outline map of North and South America and put in the main mountain ranges, deserts, jungle, great rivers, and lakes.

2 How do you suppose the early Americans made fire? Try to make it the same way.

3 Can you make a stone arrowhead using only stone tools? How long did it take you? Have you ever used a snare for catching animals? Explain how it is done, and see how many different kinds your class can make.

4 Visit a museum, if there is one, and ask to see the Stone Age relics. What was the name of the Indians who lived in your country? Ask the Curator to explain the meaning of the word *midden* and to show you any relics that have been found in middens. What can middens tell us about how people lived?

5 How many reasons can you think of why people might leave their country? Why do people migrate from your country? Why do others come to your country?

6 What was the population of the Americas when the Spaniards came? Try and find the total population today. Why do you think there has been an increase? What is the total population of your country?

7 Draw a picture showing the early Americans crossing the Bering Straits, or hunting the hairy mammoth.

8 What conditions are necessary for successful farming? Do you think the Eskimos were farmers? Why?

9 How does geography affect how people live? Why would geography have prevented some of the Indians from building in stone?

10 Can you think of any similarities between life for the early Indians and life in the Caribbean today?

CHAPTER THREE

The hunters

A traveller throughout the Americas before the arrival of the Europeans would have noticed that most of the Indians, outside the great urban areas, depended upon hunting or fishing for their subsistence. This was true of people as widely separated as the Eskimo of the Arctic, the Sioux who lived on the central plains of North America, and the Caribs of the West Indies.

The Eskimos or Inuit

For the *Eskimo* who settled in the far and frozen northlands above 60 degrees latitude, farming was impossible. The temperature for most of the year is below minus 10°C, and water freezes at 0°C. This means that not only lakes and rivers, but also the water in the soil itself freezes, so that the earth is too hard for planting. Even in the brief summer the weather is not warm enough to thaw out the soil so that plants can take root. The Eskimo, therefore, was (and is) forced to depend upon hunting and fishing for his food supply. Fortunately the Arctic abounds in meat and fish – caribou, bear, walrus, whale, salmon, deer, and especially seal, the Eskimo's favourite food.

The intense cold of the Arctic, the immense distances between settlements, and the sparse population in this vast area which stretches from *Alaska* to east of *Hudson's Bay*, determined the way in which the Eskimo organised his hunting. Let us follow Inuk (the Eskimo name for himself, meaning 'The Man') upon a typical hunting trip.

The trip begins very early in the bitter cold morning. Inuk crawls out of his *igloo* and loads his sledge or *quamuting* with food for the day. He must take enough for himself and his dogs. On the sledge also go his hunting implements, including the *harpoon*. The sledge itself is about 4 metres long × $\frac{3}{4}$ metre wide, with two runners connected with crossbars of bone or wood. Under the front crossbar a hole is drilled, through which is drawn the line which fastens the dogs' traces to the sledge. Once the sledge is loaded, and the dogs are harnessed to it, Inuk climbs on a pile of skins at the back, swings his twenty-foot whip over the dogs' heads, and steers the heavy sledge by drawing his right foot along the snow.

Inuk's goal is a 'blow-hole', a space beneath the ice where seals live and where they come to the

Seal-hunting through a blow-hole.

Sea-fishing by kayak. Notice the floats carried on the back of the boats. The fishermen will use these to mark the position of their catches.

surface to 'blow', or breathe. Approaching the hole he halts, dismounts from the sledge, and turns it upside down so that the dogs cannot draw it away. He builds a semicircular wall of snow blocks around the blow-hole, to protect himself against the wind and cold as he patiently sits waiting for signs that seals are below. In order to keep himself from moving around and so warning the seal of his presence, he ties his legs together. Then, placing his snow knife at his right hand, and his *unang*, or harpoon, at his left, he keeps a sharp eye for any movement which indicates the presence of seal. Once he knows a seal is below, he springs to his feet, and hurls his harpoon deftly into the blow-hole. The ivory point slips from the shaft as it enters the seal's body, and Inuk draws the catch to the surface.

In summer, when the sea has melted, Inuk is able to fish. For this purpose he builds a special kind of boat called a *kayak*. This is about 12 metres long, made of skins stretched over a driftwood or whalebone frame. The skins are first wetted and then stretched tightly over the frame, so that when they dry and shrink the boat is nearly waterproof. The front and back of the kayak are covered with skins, leaving only a small cockpit in which Inuk sits, with only the upper part of his body exposed. Using a double-bladed paddle he then propels himself to within throwing distance of his prey which he kills with his harpoon.

For hunting large animals like the whale, however, the Eskimo use a larger boat which they call the *umiak*, or family boat, though the word *umiak* means 'woman's boat'. This is made of a framework of wood and whalebone lashed together and covered with walrus skin. It has three or four seats, and is powered by oars, usually handled by the women of the family. Sometimes as many as three or four women are needed to handle one oar. Sometimes, too, the *umiak* has a sail. While the women row the men watch eagerly for signs of a whale. The most important member of the crew is the harpooner, upon whose skill the success of the expedition depends.

The whale is vital to the Eskimo. It provides many of the necessities of his life, such as meat and blubber for light and fuel, and hide for boats and bones to be used in place of wood in a land where wood is scarce. Traditionally, the main task of the Inuit woman to convert her husband's catch into the necessities of life – food, fuel and clothing.

However, Inuit life is vastly different today. No longer do the Inuit depend on hunting the seal and whale for food and clothing, nor do most of them live in igloos. Today most Inuit live in settled villages in permanent wooden houses, and combine traditional occupations with more modern ones. Today's Inuits might be mechanics, doctors, teachers, artists or even rock musicians!

The Sioux

Much further south, on the great plains of America, another Indian people, the *Sioux*, also lived by hunting. Their quarry was the mighty buffalo. Like the Eskimo they depended upon the success of the hunt for their food and clothing, and in addition they depended upon the buffalo to provide the skins for their *tipis* or tents. These consisted of three or four poles tied together at the top, with the bottoms forming a circle about $3\frac{1}{2}$ metres in diameter. This framework was covered with buffalo skins. Perhaps as many as twenty skins were used, sewn with bone needles and animal sinews. Designs were often painted at the bottom of the *tipi* by persons especially trained in this craft.

Tipis such as these were the typical home of the Sioux Indians. What do you think the advantages were of this sort of home for a hunting society such as the Sioux?

The all-important buffalo were hunted in the great *Buffalo Hunt* which took place annually, and was the most important event of the tribe's year. A special Chief of the Hunt was chosen, and all the braves were reminded of the rules of the hunt. Special young braves were responsible for seeing that these rules were obeyed, and disobeying these rules was one of the most serious crimes a Sioux could commit. Punishment consisted of beating the culprit, and destroying his bows and arrows and *tipi*.

The hunt itself was carefully planned. After scouts had reported on the size and whereabouts of the herd, the actual attack took place, with all the men and boys taking part. Using fire, and making a great din to frighten the animals, the hunters stampeded the mighty beasts into huge *corrals* where they were killed with arrows.

We are all very familiar with pictures of these Plains Indians riding horses. However, at the time we are now thinking about, the Indians had no horses. Horses were not introduced into the Prairies until after the Spaniards came to the New World, when they were sold to the Indians by the Spanish colonists living in what is now New Mexico and northern Mexico. Not until 1800, in fact, were all the Plains Indians fully equipped with horses. This means that the buffalo were hunted on foot by the early Indians. This was very difficult and dangerous, and explains why the discipline for the Buffalo Hunt was so strict.

In addition to the Chief of the Hunt, and the War Chief, of whom we shall read in another chapter, the Sioux had a Head Chief who led a council of forty-four assistant chiefs, including the 'medicine men' and priestly chiefs. In addition to this Council there was a sort of police force of younger braves, one of whose tasks, as we have seen, was to preserve discipline during the hunt. They were also responsible for seeing that order was kept when the tribe broke camp and travelled to its new site. After the buffalo hunt this removal was the biggest tribal event. This might happen when the hunting became meagre, and it was necessary to find new hunting grounds, or when there was too great a danger from enemy attack. During the great removal the police braves would watch out especially for theft and murder among their tribesmen. The punishment for murder was banishment from the tribe for five to ten years, a serious matter when we consider that buffalo-hunting had to be done in a large group. A man who was banished might very well starve to death, unless he could find some other tribe which was willing to accept him as a member.

The buffalo provided clothing for the Plains Indians, as well as their food and housing. For ceremonial occasions the Indians wore beautifully decorated buffalo-hide cloaks, on which were painted scenes of hunting or war. For very special occasions women embroidered the men's cloaks with porcupine quills. These embroidered cloaks were so valuable that one of the Indian tribes, the Cheyenne, had a special secret sociey which was open only to women who had made thirty such cloaks.

The Arawaks and Caribs

Much further south still, in the Caribbean, there were other Indians who also depended upon hunting and fishing for their food supply. These were the *Arawaks*, and the *Caribs*. The Arawaks were farmers, but fishing provided them with as much of their food as did farming. We know this because archaeologists have investigated the remains of their refuse tips and have found remains of many kinds of fish. Furthermore, we know that their villages were never more than five miles from the sea. We know that the Arawaks ate a great variety of fish, mainly shellfish, but also grouper, snapper, grunt, jack, parrot and barracuda. Archaeologists have found a number of oval stones with notches cut in their sides, which were

A richly-decorated buffalo-hide cloak.

probably used as sinkers for nets. In Cuba, fish were bred in artificial pools and turtles were also caught by using the *remora*, or sucker fish. The Arawak fishermen attached a line to the remora which swam alongside the canoe; then, when a turtle was seen, he slowly paid out the line until the remora had reached the turtle and attached itself to its shell by means of a powerful sucker at the top of its head. The fisherman then paddled slowly up to the turtle, drawing in his line as he did so, and lifted it into his canoe as the remora relaxed its hold. Nooses, snares and nets were used for catching birds, and part of an Arawak boy's education no doubt consisted in learning to imitate the cries of birds, and to make snares and nets. To catch waterbirds, hunters would cut eye-holes in gourds and swim slowly with these on their heads. As the birds were not likely to be disturbed by floating gourds, the hunters were able to get close enough to pull them under the water.

Although there were no large land animals in the Caribbean, the Arawaks did some hunting for what animals there were. The *hutia*, or coney, was a favourite prey. Armed with clubs, and carrying torches, the men would chase the *hutia* at night, frightening it with shouts and the flame of their torches into running toward a corral which they had built. There they killed it with their clubs. The giant lizard, or *iguana*, they caught by imitating its cry and then, when it opened its mouth to respond, jamming something inside its jaws to prevent it biting while they plucked it off the tree. These, plus the yellow snake and the *manatee*, gave the Arawaks a great variety of meat to help vary their diet.

Like the Arawaks, the Caribs were expert fishermen, who used hooks and darts made of bone, and travelled considerable distances in their wooden dug-out canoes called *piragas*. In addition to using lines and harpoons, the Caribs also sometimes used a certain wood which they bruised and threw into the water when the sea was calm. This released a poison which killed a great many fish. However, this method was seldom used, as it was wasteful as they only wanted enough food to eat. Furthermore, it was harmful to the environment.

Things to do and think about

1 Draw a picture of *either* an Eskimo or a Sioux hunt and be able to explain what is happening.

2 Are dugout canoes made anywhere in your country? Find out how they are made. What kind of trees are used? How are the trees cut? How do you suppose the Arawaks and Caribs cut their trees?

3 Some people use *kayaks* for sport. Try to see one and compare it with a dugout canoe. What prevents a *kayak* from sinking?

4 What is meant by the term 'balanced diet'? What items are missing from the diet of the hunters and fishermen you have read about?

5 Make a model of a *tipi* or try to make some quill embroidery using chicken feathers.

6 Describe how fishermen catch fish using a harpoon. Do they use it in deep water or shallow water?

7 Explain how the hunters described in this chapter showed skill in using the material at hand. Why do you think that these people built no great civilisations, or permanent buildings? What would you expect their idea of heaven to be?

8 Draw a map to show where the Indians described in this chapter lived.

9 What does the word *corral* mean? What word is used in your country for corral?

10 Find out about the following: seals, whales, buffalo, manatee, iguana, coney.

11 Write to the Inuit Tapisarat, 176 Gloucester Street, Ottawa ONT K2POA6, Canada and ask for information on present day Inuit life.

CHAPTER FOUR

The farmers

Agriculture was very important to many of the Indians of the Americas. However, the development of agriculture was influenced by the fact that the Indians had no knowledge of the wheel, or of the use of iron. Nor did they have any horses or other draught animals. The result was that most farms were very small, and the land was tilled with tools made of stone, bone or wood. The Indians never learnt to use the plough. Their most widespread tool was the digging stick, which the Maya called a *coa*. It was a pointed stick made of fire-hardened wood, and was used for making holes in the ground into which seeds were planted. The Inca version of the digging stick had a curved handle and a foot rest. They also used a wooden spade called a *taccla* and a club with a stone ring fastened to the end with which the farmers broke up clods of earth.

With these relatively simple tools, some of the Indians practised very skilful agriculture, which provided them with surplus food for times of distress. Before we consider these skilled agriculturalists, however, let us look at some other typical farming practices.

Subsistence farmers of North America

Most of the North American tribes, such as the Iroquois of the north-eastern United States and Canada, the Creeks of the southern United States, as well as the Arawaks, were subsistence farmers, using what is called the '*slash and burn*' method. This means that they burnt the land in order to clear it of weeds and bush, and cut down the trees in order to clear space for planting. The burning produced a certain amount of ash to be used as fertilizer, but it also burnt out the essential elements in the top soil, and so reduced its fertility. In addition, as these primitive farmers did not practise crop rotation, the land was quickly worn out. Among the Iroquois, for instance, it was necessary to move to a new site about every ten years, as the land could not produce enough to feed the population for longer. Among almost all the Indians it was the custom to divide agricultural work into men's and women's tasks. The men were responsible for clearing the land and breaking up the soil, while women were responsible for planting, and caring for the growing crops.

The Iroquois farmed on a large scale, growing many varieties of corn, bean and squash. They called these crops 'Our Supporters' and felt they were guarded by three spirit sisters, to whom they paid special homage. In the spring, all the women went out under a female overseer and planted the fields of each family in turn. During the ripening season both men and women performed religious ceremonies, the women dancing and singing, to ensure an abundant harvest. Harvesting took place in the Fall, when the women reaped the corn, which they husked communally.

The actual planting techniques of the Indians were very simple. Among the Arawaks, for example, the women worked in rows, each woman carrying a bag of soaked grain around her neck. She made a hole with her digging stick, threw a few grains of corn into it with her left hand, covered the whole with her foot, and repeated the process until her share of the planting was finished. If the crop was cassava (also called *yucca* or *manioc*) she cut slips from the stem and

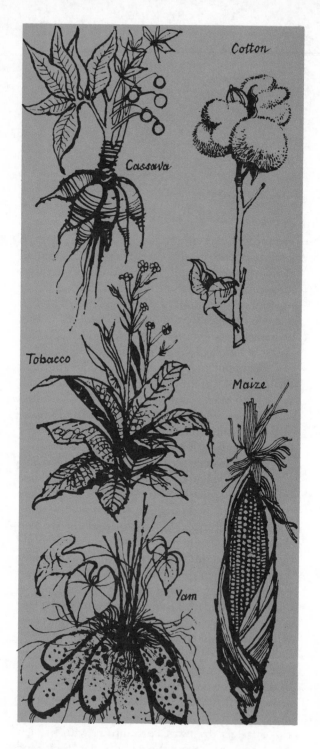

Cotton

Cassava

Tobacco

Maize

Yam

Some of the crops grown by the early peoples of the Caribbean.

planted them in mounds on level earth. Fish and ash fertiliser mixed with the soil helped to prolong its fertility. The Arawaks also seem to have known something of irrigation; in Cuba and Hispaniola irrigation trenches have been found.

In fact, there is evidence that some of the Arawak tribes practised a very intensive type of agriculture which made it possible to support quite large villages. The principle technique of this type of agriculture was called the *cunoco*. This involved heaping the soil into mounds, sometimes knee high and several feet in diameter. In each mound were planted a variety of crops in such a way as to enrich and protect one another. For example, in one such mound might be planted such root crops as cassava, along with upright crops such as corn, and climbing plants like beans. Planting such a combination of crops in one mound helped to let air into the soil and to provide ground cover, which lessened the chance of soil erosion in heavy tropical rains.

However, Arawak agriculture suffered from a problem common to most tropical areas. It was difficult to store and keep large quantities of food over a long period of time without spoilage, or infestation by insects. Hence, despite some good agricultural practices, they could not provide enough food to maintain very large populations such as were typical of the Maya, Aztec and Inca civilisations.

Not all the Arawak tribes practised such sophisticated agriculture, however. Some used a slash and burn technique, changing their fields every few years and burning out new clearings from the forest. Cassava was planted twice a year when the soil was damp, and corn was planted on hillsides during the period of the new moon and after the start of the rains. During the growing season children were stationed on platforms in trees near fields to scare away the birds.

Corn and cassava were important crops to the Caribbean Indians. In addition they planted considerable quantities of yam, several varieties of beans, and, according to the Spaniards, great quantities of cotton, as well as tobacco.

As we shall see in a later chapter the Caribs were primarily fighters and not farmers, so their agricultural techniques were generally simple. They maintained small cultivations on the islands which they inhabited. It is possible that much of the agricultural work was carried out by Arawak women captured in war.

Advanced farming techniques of the Maya, Aztec and Inca

Subsistence farming like that of the Arawaks represents one type of agriculture practised in the Americas. The highly civilised Maya, Aztec and Inca peoples, however, had developed far more advanced farming methods. Among them we find strict regulations about the ownership and use of land, and careful plans for the storing of surplus food and distributing it in times of need. This was possible because the staple crop among these Indians was corn, which can be stored for some time.

Among these Indians there was no such thing as private ownership of land. Land did not belong to individuals, but to the whole tribe or clan as a gift from God. Among the Inca, all land belonged to the Lord Inca. With the Iroquois, all farming land was owned by women. In some cases, too, a good part of the land was reserved for the leaders and the priests. It was worked by the ordinary citizens, as a part of their taxes, and the produce was used to feed the government officials (what we would call the Civil Service) and the army, as well as the priests and the ruler's family. Surplus was stored against time of scarcity when it was distributed free of cost.

Among the Maya, each married man and his wife was entitled to only four hundred square feet of land, called a *hun uinic*. Surplus grains or other non-perishable crops were collected and stored in underground storehouses called *chultunes*. A puzzling aspect of Maya agriculture is that, although today the Yucatan peninsula is dry or riverless, there is no evidence that the Maya ever practised irrigation.

The Aztec, on the other hand, had a ready-made irrigation system. Their city was built on a lake. Their problem was to create enough land to supply food for their large population. Large reed baskets were filled with earth and anchored in the shallow water of the lake. These baskets, or *chinampas*, were kept in position by surrounding

them with wooden stakes, as you can see in the picture. Thousands of these *chinampas* clustered round the city and so enlarged the Aztec's farming area. They looked like 'floating gardens'.

As with the Maya, the Aztec farming land belonged to the clan, and each clan distributed land to its own members. It was then allotted to heads of families, with one important condition: that if it was not used for two years, the clan could take it back, and give it to other families. At a

Aztec farmers cultivating their floating gardens.

These flower-filled boats at Xochimilco in Mexico remind tourists of the more practical floating gardens of the past.

man's death the land went to his sons, who had a right to its use, but did not own it. Certain lands were reserved as public lands to provide for the ruler, officials, and army, and once a year the Emperor distributed food from these lands to all the people as a sign of royal kindness.

The Inca Empire consisted of three different geographical regions: the coastal plain, much of which was desert; the steep and towering Andes Mountains, and the eastern jungle. On the Pacific Coast were a number of quite large river valleys which were made productive by means of irrigation. One canal was one hundred and twenty kilometres long. In these coastal regions, too, *guano* manure (obtained from the droppings of sea-birds), and fish heads were widely used as fertiliser. Farming on the steep slopes of the Andes required quite different methods, however. There, by means of terracing, the Inca farmers carved farms out of the mountainside. (See the picture on this page.)

For the Inca farmers, the year was divided into a rainy and a dry season. The rainy season lasted from December to March, and the dry season from April to November. Before the first ground-breaking in August, there was a festival, during which the Lord Inca ceremonially broke the first ground with a golden digging stick.

This marked the start of agricultural activity for the year. Husbands and wives worked in pairs to dig and plant the strip of land devoted to the priesthood, which they had to work on before they could attend to their own. The period between planting and harvest was devoted to weeding the growing crops. If necessary a small hut was built near the field, especially when the young corn was in danger from birds. Finally, in January, the first maize was ready for harvesting. Working as a team the members of the *ayllu* would harvest first the Emperor's and priests' fields, and then their own. The *ayllu* was the small group, or clan, to which every Inca belonged, and it was the *ayllu*, not the individual, who owned the land. All members of an *ayllu* worked on the land, picking the corn and husking it. There were two government storehouses in each province, and one in each large city, including *Cuzco*, the capital. An interesting fact to note is that this government grain was not only used in time of distress. Because of the varied climate and products in Peru, the Lord Inca ordered that whenever there was over-production of any crop in one province some of the surplus should be distributed among distant provinces, so that the people could enjoy a more varied diet.

Let us stop here for a moment, and see the importance to the world of the crops grown in the Americas. Some people have said that nearly half of all the important foods eaten in the world today originated in the Americas. Here are some of them: corn; potato; yam; squash; many varieties of bean; peanut; cashew; pineapple; cocoa; pear; tomato; pepper; pawpaw.

Terrace cultivation by Inca farmers. Notice how one farmer is channelling water on to his piece of land. Imagine you are a hill farmer. Try and invent a system for watering your land.

Agriculture and religion

Because the growing of crops was so important to the Indians, we need not be surprised to learn that there were religious ceremonies connected with agriculture, and that many of the gods had to do with farming or the weather.

The Maya, for instance, had *cenotes* or great water-holes formed by breaking away the limestone crust of rock and exposing the underground pools and streams underneath. Most Maya cities of the riverless Yucatan peninsula had two of these *cenotes*. One was used to supply water. The other was used as a sacrificial well into which young girls were ceremonially thrown in order, as the Maya thought, to bring rain.

The Inca, too, had special religious festivities connected with agriculture. As we have seen, the fields reserved for the priesthood were the first to be planted. From the planting, until the appearance of the first sprouts, the Priests of the Sun fasted and prayed for a good harvest. Then, at the beginning of the rainy season, another important ceremony took place. The arrival of rain was awaited with great anxiety, and the gods, especially the God of Thunder, were implored to send the life-giving showers. People dressed themselves in mourning and marched weeping through the streets. Black llamas and dogs were tied up without water, in the hope that their cries of hunger and thirst would reach the ears of the gods and hasten the rain. When at last the rains came, the event was celebrated once again with singing and dancing. Throughout the entire Inca Empire there were shrines, called *huacas*, for sacrifice to the gods and especially the gods of agriculture. Successful farming meant life for the people, and peace in the Empire.

Among the Iroquois and Creek Indians the great religious festival was the *Green Corn Ceremony*. This took place in August when the corn was at the roasting stage. No one was permitted to eat any corn before the ceremony took place. During the Green Corn Ceremony, the Creeks forgave anyone who had wronged them during the year.

So in their different ways, most of the Indians developed a life based on agriculture. And, as we shall see, those who were able to produce a surplus of food, developed complex civilisations.

Things to do and think about

1 Explain the meaning of 'slash and burn' agriculture. Do any farmers in your country use this method?

2 What are the main agricultural tools your farmers use? What advantages do farmers today have over those of the early Indian farmers?

3 Compare the Indian attitude toward land use and land ownership with ours. Is there anything regarding land use which we can learn from the Indians? Be prepared to discuss your answer.

4 Make a fire-hardened digging stick, and use it to plant something in the school garden. How does a digging stick compare with the cutlass or hoe?

5 Find out in what ways your government is trying to improve land use.

6 What crops have been brought into your territory from other countries? Which crops are native to your country?

7 What are the best conditions for growing corn, cocoa, 'Irish' potato, cassava? Which of these are grown in your country? In what parts of the country do they grow best? Why?

8 Try to make a small *chinampa*. How long did it take to build up enough soil for planting?

9 Find out all you can about the geography, e.g. climate, rainfall, and topography of the Yucatan peninsula; the Valley of Mexico; the West Coast of Peru; the Andes.

10 What religious festivals are observed in your territory in connection with agriculture?

CHAPTER FIVE

The warriors

The America Columbus found was not a peaceful place. It is true that there were no long wars which continued for many years, nor were the armies large. Yet war played an important part in the lives of most of the Indians. Some of them felt that success in battle was the only road to power and glory. This was true of the Iroquois, the Sioux and the Caribs. But it was also true of the Aztec, though for a different reason.

The Indians knew little of the use of metal, and they had no knowledge at all of gunpowder. Therefore their weapons consisted of those which could be made from wood, bone, or stone. They

This young Inca warrior carries a bolas and a finely-made sling.

used war clubs, which sometimes had star-shaped heads made of bronze, which the Maya called *macana*; and bows and arrows, which the Caribs poisoned, so that even a scratch was fatal; and wooden swords; and knives made of sharp rock. The Aztec used the throwing-spear which they were able to hurl great distances by using an *atlatl*, or grooved throwing stick. Among the Inca, a favourite weapon was the sling made of fibre, which was six inches long. They used it to hold their hair in place when they were not fighting. The Inca soldiers also used the *bolas* which consisted of three stones, each fastened to a cord which were then tied together and thrown at the enemy. Many of the Indians also used very simple weapons like fire arrows, which quickly set fire to the thatched roofs of their enemies' houses. The Maya even used hornets' nests, which they hurled into enemy villages in order to spread confusion.

The Indians, naturally, also developed some protection against these weapons. The Sioux, Iroquois and Maya used wooden shields which the Maya decorated with feathers and called *chimalli*. The Aztec and Inca wore a kind of armour made of quilted cotton soaked in brine, which became very hard, and offered protection against clubs and wooden swords. They also wore helmets made of wood.

In addition to these colourful costumes, the Indians decorated their bodies and painted their faces before going into battle. Among the Aztec there were two groups of warriors who were held in special honour and wore an outstanding head dress. These were known as *Jaguar knights*, who wore the skin of a jaguar into battle, and *Eagle knights*, whose helmet was an eagle's head. Only

Aztec warriors. Their elaborate headgear was designed to frighten the enemy.

exceptionally brave soldiers could be jaguar or eagle knights, and only these knights could wear head dresses made of the gorgeously coloured feathers of the *quetzal* bird.

For special courage in battle, Indian warriors were also awarded medals. The Caribs wore a crescent-shaped copper medal around their necks, which they called *caracolis*, and which they greatly prized. Among the Inca, the highest ranking officers wore gold medals, while the ordinary soldiers wore copper.

Training the young warriors

Let us now see something of Indian methods of fighting their battles. Because success in war was a sign of manhood among the Iroquois, Sioux and Carib, each boy in these tribes was trained from birth to be a warrior. Much of a boy's education consisted in teaching him how to make and use his weapons, and hardening him for the test of skill and courage that was to come. Whenever a Sioux boy, for example, was successful in a shooting contest with his friends, his father would give a feast at which all the relatives and friends of the family made speeches in which they predicted a great future for the boy as a warrior. Carib boys were trained by being made to shoot their meals down from the top of trees in order to improve their marksmanship, and to shoot accurately while swimming. Before a Carib boy could become a warrior he had to undergo a severe initiation ceremony. When the day came, he was seated on a stool before all the warriors of his village, while his father explained to him what his duties and responsibilities would be in the future. Then a bird was beaten to death against his body, scratching and pecking at his skin as it struggled. After this he was deeply scratched with agouti teeth, and his body was rubbed with the dead bird which meantime had been dipped in hot pepper. During all of this the boy was expected to show no sign of pain or discomfort. When the beating was over, he was given the bird's heart to eat, and then was sent to his hammock and made to fast. Only when he successfully passed through this initiation was he given a warrior's name, taught the warrior's language, and allowed to go on raids.

Fighting for plunder

In all societies it was common for warriors to have special rituals to prepare for war. Before a raid, both the Iroquois and Sioux warriors would fast, and would not eat again until the raid was over. As raids were very short, this was not too difficult to do. The night before they went on the raid, the warriors spent the time in dancing and singing, and decorating their bodies with warpaint. The Iroquois would carry out their raid only if the *shamans*, or priests, dreamt that it would be a success. Even when the war party was on its way, if anyone dreamed it would fail, the party turned back, and waited until the *shemans*, or one of the warriors dreamed it would be successful. The Caribs on the other hand, worked themselves into a rage before setting out on an attack and would never turn back once they had started. Like people everywhere, these Indians felt they had good reasons for fighting. The Caribs fought mainly to get food and women from their weaker neighbours. The Plains Indians invaded the territory of other tribes in their pursuit of the buffalo. The Iroquois' first wars were fought in order to seize land from neighbours.

The Caribs were a seafaring people who attacked from canoes. These canoes, or *piragas*, sometimes held over fifty men and travelled very swiftly. Their attacks, mainly directed against the peaceful Arawaks, were sudden, and very brutal. Often they began with a shower of fire arrows which set their enemies' thatched houses alight. Then, leaping from their canoes, the Caribs

savagely clubbed and shot their way to victory. When the fighting was over, the victors piled the bodies of their dead into their canoes, for they refused to leave their dead and wounded behind. In the canoes, too, were the men and women they had taken prisoner. Before returning home, the canoes sailed along the coasts while the Carib warriors sang songs of triumph and shouted insults at their defeated enemy.

When the warriors returned home, the captives were shared out. Women were kept as slaves, or given to the young men as wives. The men, however, were carried to their captor's house where they were tied up and starved for four to five days. At the end of that time, there was a great

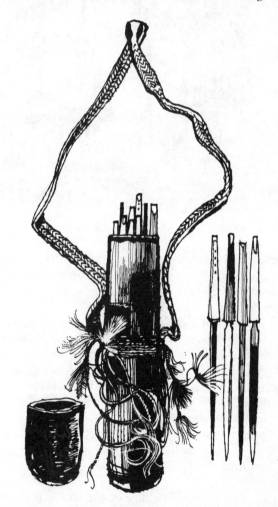

A Carib arrow-quiver. The case was used to carry poisoned arrowheads.

remony, in which the captured men were tortured to death, and then ceremonially eaten by members of the tribe. The Caribs believed that in doing this they increased their power, by adding their enemies' strength to their own. It was partly because they were cannibals that the Caribs were so feared.

Among the North American Indians the war parties were often smaller than the Caribs, sometimes as few as five warriors taking part, but the attacks were just as sudden. Like the Caribs, too, the North Americans tortured their prisoners to death in their victory celebrations. In each of their villages was a torturing pole to which the victims were tied, and put to death with very great cruelty.

We often hear about scalping among the North American Indians. This practice of cutting a piece of scalp and the scalp lock from a dead enemy was used to prove the number of men a warrior had killed. It was very common among the Sioux, and after each raid the victorious warriors took part in the *Scalp Dance*. During this dance, the warrior '*counted coup*', which means he recounted his valorous deeds during the raid, and boasted of his bravery. The bravest deed of all was to make a *coup*, to touch an enemy without killing him. Sometimes, in counting *coup*, a warrior was tempted to lie. In this case any other member of the war party could challenge him to prove his boast. Then, instead of the admiration and glory he sought, the boaster might earn only the sneers and scorn of his tribesmen. Even boys too young to take part in raids were encouraged to take part in the scalp dance, and to boast of the mighty deeds they would accomplish in the future. Then they were praised, and in this way were encouraged to think of themselves as already being warriors.

Fighting for new lands

So far we have read only about those Amerindians who fought for the sake of plunder. The Inca fought for a different reason. They fought wars of conquest, to gain new lands. The Inca were the best organised of all the Indian soldiers, and they were the only Indians whose armies could undertake long campaigns far from home. The map on

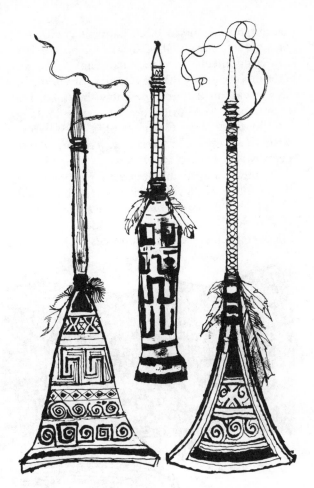

These Carib clubs were used on ceremonial occasions.

p. 43 will show you the tremendous area the Inca armies were able to conquer. This was possible because they were able to put very large numbers of soldiers in the field. Also, the Inca built excellent roads, so that soldiers and supplies could be moved quickly and easily throughout the empire.

We have seen in the last chapter how the Inca stored grain in royal granaries. Part of this was used to feed the army. These granaries were built so that there was always one within a day's march, which meant that the armies need never go short of food. In this way strict discipline was maintained, for the Inca soldier did not have to forage for food in the countryside and so molest the civilian population. Any soldier who foraged for food was severely punished.

Another reason why the Inca armies were so successful was that the soldiers did not desert when

23

harvest time came as often happened with the Maya, for example. The Inca soldiers were all conscripts; that is, every Inca male had to give, for a time, compulsory military service. But while he was serving in the army he knew that the other members of his district, or *ayllu*, were looking after his fields. This was quite unlike the situation with the Caribs and North Americans, where every warrior was a volunteer.

As the Inca armies conquered new territories, they built great fortified cities to protect their conquests. One of these was *Macchu Picchu*, which was so well hidden high in the Andes that it was discovered only by chance, hundreds of years after the Spanish conquest of Peru. The great fortress of *Sacsahuaman*, which was built to protect the inhabitants of *Cuzco*, the capital, was defended by stone walls twenty metres high. One of the stone blocks used to build the wall weighed over one hundred tons.

The Inca were not the only Indians who required their young men to give military service. The Aztec, too, trained their boys to serve in the army. In fact, they had special schools called *telpuchcalli*, or *houses of youth*, to which all boys were sent at the age of fifteen. Here they were trained in the duties of a citizen, as well as in the arts of war. The teachers in these schools were a

Sacsahuaman as it might have been. Twenty-five thousand men worked constantly on the construction of this great fortress. It was completed in eighty years.

nowned warriors who had captured an enemy
battle. Boys remained at the *telpuchcalli* until
ey, too, had captured an enemy. Then they were
ee to leave the school and marry. While a boy
as at the *telpuchcalli* he wore a plait at the back of
s head which was cut off when he had captured
s first prisoner. If he went into battle several
mes without capturing any prisoners he was
sgraced.

ighting for human sacrifice

a order to understand why the Aztec were so
axious to capture prisoners in war we must
nderstand a little about their religion. Their great
eity was *Huitzilopochtli* the 'Humming Bird
Vizard', who, according to their legends, had
hosen them to be his special people. After many
enerations of wandering he had guided them to
he site of their homeland. In order to please him
and to ensure that the sun would shine always, the
Aztec made regular sacrifices to him. This was
important, for they believed that the world had
already been created and destroyed four times, and
that the time they were living in was the fifth.
Their priests foretold that this time the world
would be destroyed by an earthquake. In order to
prevent this happening, the Aztec sought to win
their god's favour by making him a gift of the
most precious substance they knew – human
blood. Therefore they fought, not only for food
or conquest, or for revenge, but also to obtain
prisoners for sacrifice.

The Maya also sacrificed war prisoners to the
gods, but frequently their wars were fought
between the Maya cities themselves. Sometimes
they fought to gain advantages in trade, sometimes to gain more land for agriculture, sometimes
to get slaves. Often it was these slaves who were
sacrificed. However, the Maya could not fight
long wars, for as we have seen, most of them were

Sacsahuaman today. This
photograph shows part of
the remains of the fortress.
Notice how the great
blocks of stone have been
cut and fitted together.

25

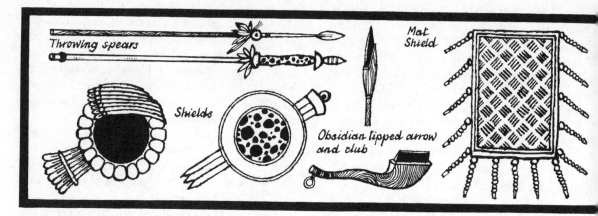

Some Maya weapons. The picture shows: (1) throwing spears, (2) and (3) round shields, (4) an arrowhead tipped with obsidian, (5) a mat shield, and (6) a stone-tipped club.

farmers, and when harvest time came they wanted to return home. Usually battles were fought in October when the farmer–soldier was not needed in his fields. They went into battle under a leader called a *nacom*, who was elected for three years. Under him were the captains, and under them the ordinary soldiers, called *holcans*. These were paid a small sum by their captains while the war lasted. Unfortunately for the Maya, they were not very disciplined soldiers. We have seen that they could not fight during harvest time. Nor would they fight at night. If their leader died in the fighting, the war ended. This was to be a great disadvantage when they came to fight the Spaniards.

Things to do and think about

1 How many reasons can you find why people go to war today? Are any of these the same as the Indians' reasons for fighting?

2 What were the names of the wars that Europeans fought for religious reasons? What other people you have read about fought for religion? Do you think that religion is a good reason for war? Why do you think so?

3 Try and make any one of the Indian weapons. Which one do you think would be most effective? Why? (To do this properly you should examine Indian weapons at your local museum, if there is one.)

4 Make up a story or play about the return of a Sioux War Party.

5 The Inca are sometimes called the Romans of the Americas. Find out what you can about the Roman army and show in what ways they were similar.

CHAPTER SIX

The Maya

For many centuries the rainforests of *Guatemala* hid a mystery as the thick vegetation hid enormous stone palaces and temples. Then in 1773, explorers stumbled across the ruins of a great building. When they cleared the bush they found the remnants of a large stone city. Other explorers and archaeologists followed, and little by little more temples and other stone buildings were discovered beneath the vegetation. These were remnants of a great Maya civilisation.

The earliest Maya lived as long ago as 2000 B.C. in a forest region known as *El Peten*. For nearly three thousand years, from 2000 B.C. until about A.D. 900, they slowly developed the arts of their civilisation. They became farmers. They learnt to make and fire clay pots. They constructed great stone buildings like the ones the explorers found, and on the walls of some of these buildings they painted murals which tell us a good deal about their lives. They had, for example, developed a calendar as accurate as the Egyptians'. As we saw in Chapter 1, when men became farmers, the priest–astronomers who could foretell the changes of weather and season became persons of importance and power. This was true of the Maya priests, and, as we shall see later, it was also true for the Aztec and the Inca. Similarly, the Maya and the Aztec Indians, like the Egyptians, built tremendous stone pyramids, although the Indian pyramid had a flat top, while those of Egypt were pointed.

In about A.D. 900 however, these cities were abandoned for some unknown reason. The inhabitants migrated to the flat, riverless limestone Yucatan peninsula. There they built new cities like *Uxmal*, *Mayapan*, and *Chichén Itzá*, and there they were living when the Spaniards came. We know a great deal about the Maya since A.D. 900, for many of their buildings and statues still stand, and the Spaniards wrote about what they saw and learnt from these people whom they conquered.

The Pyramid of Kukulcan at Chichén Itzá. The temple is at the top of the pyramid.

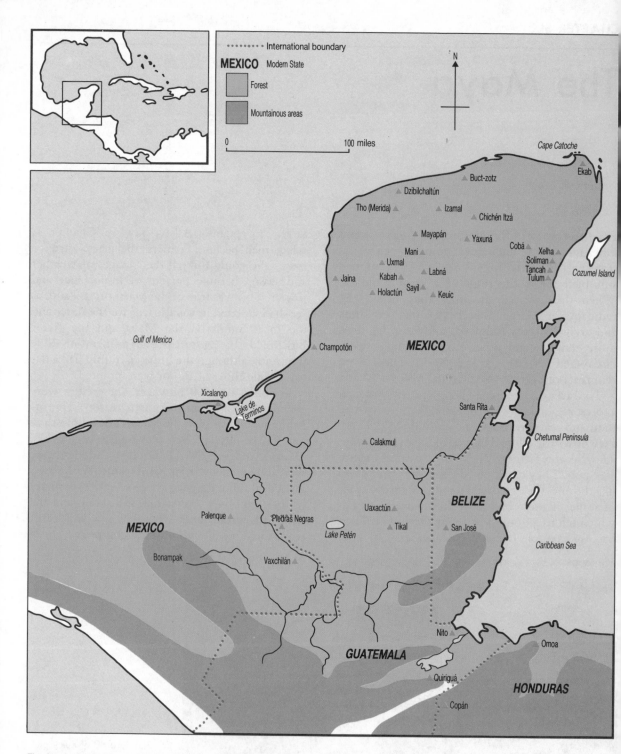

The land of the Mayas. The chief Maya sites are shown
on this map, but many more lie in unexplored jungle and
forest.

The influence of religion

We know, for example, that religion played a very great part in the life of the Maya people. Their priests played an important part in many activities, and many of their great buildings were devoted to religious purposes. For this reason we call Maya cities 'temple cities', for their outstanding buildings were the temples they built on top of the high flat-topped pyramids.

These pyramids were made with a core of earth and rubble, covered with cut stone, and then cemented with mortar made by burning limestone rock. Narrow steps led up the steep sides to a dark windowless temple. The entrance to the temple was through a *corbelled arch*. Only the priests who performed the ceremonies could enter these temples. The worshippers remained outside, in the plazas or courtyards surrounding the sacred pyramids. From here they watched the rites, and took part by singing and dancing.

These gigantic stone buildings were made with the simplest tools, for the Maya, like all American Indians, knew nothing of metal tools. Fortunately, limestone is fairly soft, and can be cut and shaped with stone tools and with sand. The usual method of quarrying stone was to drive wooden wedges into cracks in the rock and then wet the wood. As the wood swelled, the crack widened. Then the split stone was laboriously cut out with stone hammers and chisels. It has been estimated that it would have taken about 25,000 hours of work to quarry enough stone to build just one of the great Maya pyramids!

What type of religious beliefs inspired the Maya to build such impressive monuments? Like all the Indians of the Americas, they worshipped many gods. They believed that all of life was a struggle between good and evil, and that there were good and evil gods. The good gods lived in thirteen heavens, and the evil ones lived in nine hells. Great warriors, and those who were killed in sacrifice,

This wall painting of a waterside village is inside the Temple of the Warriors at Chichén Itzá. What can we learn about the daily life of the Maya from pictures like this? Try and find out what everybody is doing in the picture.

A corbelled arch. Notice how the arch is constructed using overlapping layers of stones.

The Maya as mathematicians

The Maya also built round observatories from which their priests could observe the movement of the stars and planets. Here they developed the calendars we have read about.

Let us now take a closer look at the Maya calendar. This calendar was as accurate as the one we use today, but it was divided differently. Like us, the Maya had a 365-day year. This was called a *haab*, and consisted of eighteen months or *uinals*, each of twenty days, or *kins*. This gave 360 days. The five days left over at the end were called *uayeb*, and were considered an unlucky period. However, in addition to this calendar, the Maya had two others. One, which they called the *tzolkin*, was the sacred calendar by which they reckoned the special feasts of the gods. It had 260 days. The other, which was peculiar to the Maya, was called the *long count*. This was a method of reckoning time by counting every single day from the

were sure of going to heaven. They believed in immortality, and to make sure that the dead would be able to enjoy the afterlife, they buried them with a maize drink, and the tools of their trade.

One of the most important Maya gods was the God of Corn, *Yum Kax*. Other gods were also connected with agriculture: for instance, *Chac*, the God of Rain, and *Pipil*, the God of the Sun, *Itzamna*, the Giver of Food and Light. Another important god was one who was brought to them by the *Toltecs*. The Toltecs were a highly civilised people who lived in Mexico before the Aztecs. In about A.D. 987 they arrived in the Yucatan, where by this time the Maya had settled. Toltec religious ideas became mixed with those of the Maya, and the Toltec god *Quetzalcoatl* became for the Maya *Kukulcán*, or God of the Winds. He was pictured as a feathered serpent, with fangs bared in his snarling open mouth. But above all their gods, the Maya felt that there was one who was the invisible supreme creator. They called him *Kunab Ku*. There are no pictures of Kunab Ku because he was, as already said, invisible. But many of the other gods, especially Kukulcán (and Chac, who was pictured with a long, curved, snout-like nose), were carved on their temples.

Kukulcán, the God of the Winds. The Maya based Kukulcán on the Toltec god, Quetzalcoatl.

beginning of Maya history, and when they wanted to refer to a date in the long distant past, they simply counted back one day at a time to the beginning, which for them was around 3111 B.C.

Unlike us, the Maya did not reckon their time in centuries. They believed that time was a cycle, and that what happened once would be repeated again. They counted time in two kinds of cycle: the *katun* (a period of 7,200 days – just short of twenty years); and a longer fifty-two year cycle.

Obviously the Maya had to have an accurate system of numbering to work out such a complicated and exact calendar. Their number system was based on the figure 20, and they called it 'The Whole Man' because it used all the fingers and toes. They also discovered the importance of zero,

The observatory at Chichén Itzá. The observation chamber is at the top.

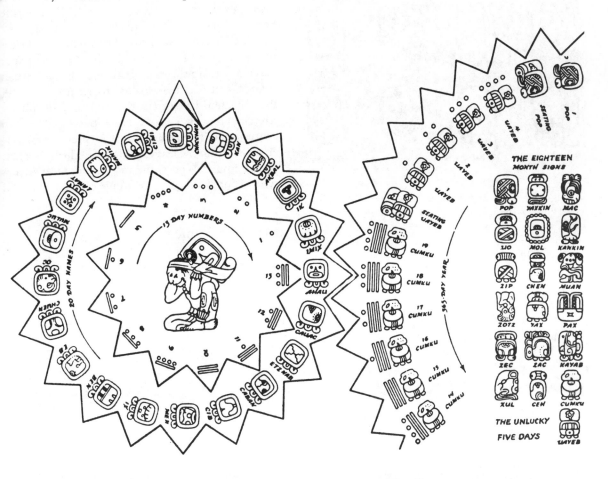

The very complicated calendar invented by the Mayas. The wheel on the left shows the sacred year of 260 days; the wheel on the right shows part of the calendar year of 365 days. The Maya calendar year contained eighteen months of twenty days each, and an unlucky period of five days.

31

Glyphs of the Maya days. Each of the twenty days in a month had a name, and each was represented by a glyph.

IMIX IK AKBAL KAN
CHICCHAN CIMI MANIK LAMAT
MULUC OC CHUEN EB
BEN IX MEN CIB
CABAN EZNAB CAUAC AHAU

which they used long before the Europeans learn about it from India. Maya numbers were written in two ways, either as dots and dashes, or as symbols or pictures. They counted from top to bottom. Each number had its own symbol or picture, except for zero which could be written in many different ways, but was usually represented by a mollusc shell. The diagram below will give you an idea of how they counted.

These numbers formed part of the Maya system of writing, which was in the form of glyphs or pictures. These were sometimes carved on huge stone monuments called *stelae*, which commemorated important events. Some of these stelae were ten metres high and weighed fifty tonnes. They were often erected at the end of the fifty-two year cycle. In addition, however, the Maya wrote books containing accounts of their history and legends. The earliest known book in the Americas was written by the Maya in A.D. 890. The paper was made from the inner bark and fibre of certain trees which was first soaked to remove the sap, then beaten to soften the fibres, and finally stretched so that each page measured 8 × 25 centimetres. The book ends were glued to wooden boards, and the leaves folded together like a fan. As we might expect, the priests were the scribes who painted the glyphs, using brushes made of wild pig bristle.

Maya government

We can see, then, that the Maya were an advanced people. How were they governed and how did

Maya numbers. Can you see how the large numbers on the right are made up?

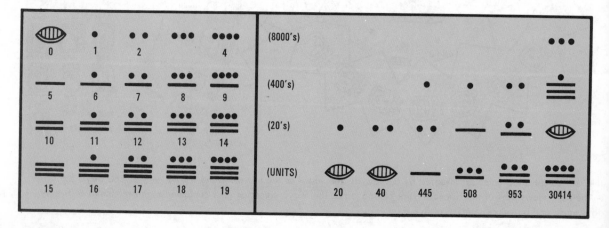

hey live? They lived in independent city-states. Their society was strictly divided into rigid classes, each of which had its own rights and duties, even in such matters as clothing and personal adornment. The ruler of each city-state was the *halach uinich* – the 'true man' or 'real man'. Unlike the ruler of the Aztec who was elected, and the Lord Inca who was selected, the *halach uinich* was a hereditary ruler. The office descended from father to son, as in European monarchies. However, if the sons of the dead ruler were not fit to rule, one of his brothers became head of state. Failing this, some other suitable person from the ruler's family was elected by a council of nobles.

After the ruler and the nobles came the majority of the people who were farmers or artisans. But there also existed a curious group known as the *ppolms*, or merchants. These merchants played a special and important role. They had their own god, and lived according to their own laws. Moreover, they did not have to pay taxes or give any personal service in agricultural labour or road building as the other commoners did. On the other hand, they performed a very important role in foreign affairs, and especially in war, for they frequently acted as spies.

In addition to this, the *ppolms* made possible the exchange of goods between the various Maya cities. The Maya were the only American Indians who carried on trade by sea as well as by land, and there is evidence that their forty-foot long canoes had some contact with Cuba and Jamaica. What

kinds of goods were traded? Salt was an important commodity and certain tribes had a monopoly of its trade. Brightly coloured feathers, used in warriors' head-dresses and as a mark of honour,

Some pages from the earliest known book in the Americas. Can you see examples of Maya glyphs and numbers? Invent your own system of writing and counting and write a message in your new language to your friends and see if they understand it!

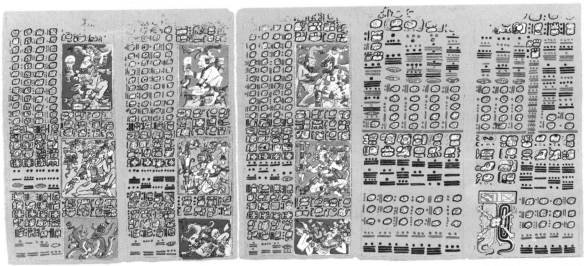

were carried from the jungle cities to the sea-coast and highland peoples. Cotton for weaving Maya garments; cocoa, which formed the favourite drink; honey, wax, fish, flint, maize, precious stones for ornaments, shells, gold-gods of all descriptions were carried by the *ppolms*. They used no money, but instead used cocoa beans as a means of exchange. A rabbit, for example, was sold for ten beans, a slave for a hundred. Sometimes small copper bells, or red shells or strings were also used as a medium of exchange.

The life of the people

The Maya also built great roadways called *sacbeobs*, to encourage trade between their various cities. Some of these roads were almost a hundred kilometres long. Where necessary the *sacbeobs* were crossed by bridges made of logs and beams. In each village were people whose duty it was to keep up a 'travellers' house' in which wood, maize, and other provisions were always available.

Maya men wore a simple cotton garment called an *ex* (pronounced eesh). This was a loincloth wound several times around the waist and passed between the legs. Over this they wore a mantle without sleeves. Sandals were tied to the feet with two thongs, and were called *keuel*. Women wore the *kub* – a simple dress with a square neck. Beneath this they wore a light petticoat. They went barefoot. However, in addition to these simple garments the nobles wore a great deal of jewelry – ear and nose rings, bracelets. Moreover, their garments and sandals were dyed in many colours, and on ceremonial occasions the noble-men would decorate themselves with feathered head-dresses made on wicker frames sometimes nearly as large as themselves. But only the ruler and outstanding warriors were permitted to use the gorgeously coloured feathers of the *quetzal* bird in their head-dresses.

Around the year A.D. 800, there were more than three million Mayas. They were short people, not much above five feet, but they were robust and strong. They were broad-headed, and as soon as a baby was born, its head was flattened still more by squeezing it gently between two boards. This, said the Maya, 'gives us a noble air . . . and besides, our heads are then better adapted to carry loads. Many Maya, whose features were (and still are) very much like those of Mongolians, were also cross-eyed. This was regarded as a special mark of beauty and distinction, and mothers would hang a ball in front of their children so that they would focus on it and so develop cross-eyes.

Maya houses were simple. Most were wattled and thatched, although the wealthier nobles might have built theirs of stone. Almost all homes, however, consisted of one room; with neither windows nor doors. Instead, across the doorway was hung a curtain and small copper bells. Furniture was very sparse, usually just sleeping racks made of saplings laced with springy branches and covered with a grass mattress and cotton blankets. Cooking was done outside by the women. Like women in most cultures Maya women were responsible for caring for the home and children. However, as happens in agricultural societies even today, they also performed a good deal of the agricultural labour, mainly sowing, weeding and reaping of crops.

Childbearing started at a very early age. A woman was supposed to produce many children. If she were barren it was considered a disgrace. This meant that from her early teens a girl married and took on adult responsibilities. As a home-maker she supplied almost all of her family's needs. For example, she wove the cloth and then sewed the garments. Moreover, she also shared responsibility with other women for making the magnificent feathered head-dresses worn by the nobility.

A major part of women's time was spent in the preparation of food for her large family. This time-consuming task involved grinding corn on a grinding stone or *metate*, then forming the meal into flat cakes, called tortillas, which were baked on clay sheets. Her stove consisted of three stones placed on the ground behind the house. Since a working man could eat twenty such tortillas a day we can imagine how much of a woman's time and energy was devoted to this one task. If her husband travelled much in his work, such as a soldier or *ppolm* might do she had the additional task of preparing a special food which could be carried for long distances without danger of spoiling. Such food, called *pinole*, consisted of corncake made of roasted cornflour mixed with honey. Unfortunately for the Mayan woman, her life was not only hard, but was often also unpleasant. She was considered an inferior person, and girls were trained from childhood to accept a subordinate place in society. A girl would notice, for example, that her mother and other women always turned their backs and stepped aside if they met a man on the road, and that when in the presence of a man, women always looked down to the ground. To look directly at a man, or worse, to laugh at him, was considered serious misconduct and was severely punished. A mother might pinch her daughter, or rub her eyes with red pepper, or beat her if the girl refused to act 'properly' toward men.

Even fully-grown women were accorded little respect. No woman might inherit a man's property – not even his mother. If a man died, his son (or, if the boy were too young, his brothers or other male relatives) inherited everything. It was then their responsibility to look after the female relatives – mother, wife and daughters.

All this and more the Spaniards saw and marvelled at when they first encountered the Maya. They described a sacred Ball Court at Chichén Itzá which was 165 metres long and 70 metres wide. There the Maya played a ball game, called *pok-a-tok*, in which the players had to butt a solid rubber ball through hoops set 10 metres above the ground. They marvelled at a country which provided no prisons and in which anyone who stole was punished by having to work off the value of his theft. They noticed with respect the skill with which the Maya provided themselves with water in their dry peninsula, by damming and cementing ravines. They marvelled, but they also conquered.

Things to do and think about

1 If you could make any changes in the life of a Maya woman, which are the most important changes you would make? Explain your choices. There are places today where one group in society is considered inferior. Find out where some of these places are, and the ways in which people are discriminated against. What reasons might be given for considering any group as inferior? Explain why you do, or do not, accept these reasons.

2 Look at the picture on page 29. What does it tell us about life in a Maya village?

3 The Maya burnt trees to make lime for cement; this eventually contributed to the disappearance of forest in the Yucatan. Find out all you can about afforestation in your country and why it is undertaken.

4 Find out what you can about the making of roads in the Maya Empire. How did the Roman roads compare with the Mayan *sacbeobs*?

5 Like the Maya, the Greek peoples also organised themselves into city-states. Find out what you can about the Greek city-states, and see how they compared with the Maya.

6 Maya civilisation is also similar to that of the ancient Egyptians. Find out what you can about ancient Egypt, so that you can compare the two civilisations.

7 What did the Maya learn from the Toltecs? In what ways do people learn from other nations, and why do they do so? Discuss this statement: 'Influence from outside is not always good.' How does the statement apply to outside influences in your country?

8 Try to do a simple sum using Maya numbers. Is it easier or more difficult than using our Arabic numbers?

9 Find out all you can about life in Guatemala and the Yucatan Peninsula today, and paste this information into your scrapbook.

CHAPTER SEVEN

The Aztec

In Chapter 6, we saw how the Toltec god, *Quetalcoatl*, became part of the Maya religion. The Toltec were a highly civilised people who lived in the Valley of Mexico. Their capital was at *Tula*, not far from present-day *Mexico City*. In about 1156, however, their lands were invaded by the more savage Aztec. By A.D. 1325 the Aztec (also known as the *Mexica* or *Tenochca*) had built a

settlement on a swampy island in *Lake Texcoco* They called it *Tenochtitlán*. According to Aztec legend they were led to this place by their god *Huitzilopochtli*, who directed their priests to look for a place where they would see an eagle on a cactus in a lagoon holding a snake in its beak.

From humble beginnings the Aztec built them-selves a great empire, and made their city which

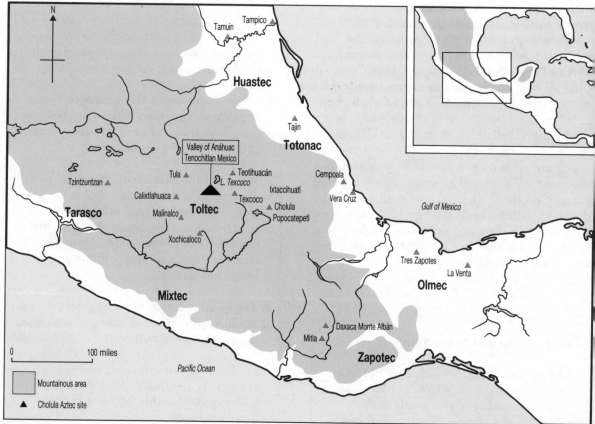

The Land of the Aztecs.

was built on water, one of the wonders of the Americas. As they became more settled, their kings added to the city, by building an aqueduct to bring fresh water, and by building defences against flood waters from the lake. Little by little the Aztec kings conquered their neighbours, until they controlled the great area you can see on the map.

One of the greatest Aztec conquerors was *Moctezuma II*, who was ruling when news came of the arrival in *Vera Cruz*, of strange beings of a light colour who walked on four legs. Wondering who these might be, Moctezuma sent them gifts, and a message to come to Tenochtitlán. These strange men turned out to be the Spaniards! So Cortez and his men found their way to the Aztec capital, and wrote down for us the wonders of the Aztec Empire.

The Spaniards were amazed at the magnificent city they beheld. High in the mountains of the Mexican plateau, surrounded by smoking volcanoes, Tenochtitlán's white buildings gleamed in the bright sunshine. Three great causeways, each wide enough for eight people to walk abreast, connected the island city to the mainland. The city itself had no streets, but used instead footpaths of beaten earth which ran alongside canals. The canals carried the heavy traffic in canoes, while pedestrians, and porters carrying loads to and from the markets, used the pathways. The city was wonderfully clean to the Spaniards' eyes, for it was kept dry by means of underground drains, while stone-lined underground sewers carried off waste. At various points along the canals special canoes were sent to collect any offal and refuse, which was then carried off to be used as fertiliser.

The centre of the city consisted of a great plaza, above which towered a great pyramid on top of which was built the twin temples to *Huitzilopochtli*, the God of War, and *Tlaloc*, the God of Rain. In the square before the great pyramid was also to be seen a raised platform on which gladiators fought. A skull rack stood nearby, and not far off were smaller temples to lesser gods. In contrast to the crowded causeways and cheerful market, the square was a brooding place, silent before the implacable Aztec gods.

Training young leaders

Not far from the centre of the city were the famous Aztec schools, the *calmecac* and the *telpochcalli* about which we read in Chapter 5. The *telpochcalli* were attended by the majority of boys but the *calmecac* were special schools for training priests and high officials, who were to be future leaders. A large *calmecac* might contain a hundred boys, who remained there for eight to ten years from the age of fifteen. There they were taught to read and write Aztec hieroglyphics and to calculate the complicated Aztec calendar. In addition they were taught Aztec history and law, agriculture and the art of war. Above all, they were taught the songs, dances and sacrificial rites through which the Aztec gods were served. Discipline in the *calmecac* was very strict, and boys who were disobedient, or careless in their work and speech were punished by being pricked with maguey spines which older boys had gathered from the mountains during the night.

Moctezuma II, King of the Aztecs.

Girls were also sent to school at fifteen, where they were taught by priestesses. For them, too, discipline was very strict. They were not allowed to talk at meals, and had to sit in silence for long periods. Most of their teaching had to do with homemaking, and when they left school most girls got married. However, a few special ones were kept on to be trained as priestesses.

Religion and learning

The Aztec worshipped many gods. They believed, as we read in Chapter 5, that human sacrifice was necessary to please these powerful beings. One of their most important religious ceremonies was called the *New Fire Ceremony*. This took place at the end of their fifty-two year cycle. Its purpose was to please the gods so that they would allow the people to exist for another fifty-two year cycle.

At the start of the New Fire Ceremony everyone cleaned their house thoroughly, smashed old pottery and utensils, and put out all fires. Each priest, dressed in the costume of the god he represented, left Tenochtitlán, and walked slowly to the top of the sacred *Hill of the Star*. There they waited in silence until the sacred star had reached a certain spot in the heavens. When that happened, a priest quickly kindled the new fire, and thrust into it the heart of a special sacrificial victim. When this had been done, a great bonfire was lit, from which priests of all the Aztec towns kindled their torches which they carried swiftly back to the waiting people. Each family relit its fire thankfully, and renewed its household goods and clothing and ornaments, amidst much feasting and rejoicing.

Boys in the *calmecac* were taught not only to perform sacrificial rites, but also to be able to calculate, and to interpret the Aztec calendar. This was important, for each god had his special days and months, and certain days were felt to be unlucky. If a child was born on an unlucky day, his parents might ask the priest to postpone naming him until a more lucky date.

Aztec writing, like the Maya, was in the form of *hieroglyphics*. They wrote on a paper called *amatl*, which was made from the inner bark of the wild Ficus tree. This was first soaked, and then beaten with a stone to soften the fibres. It was then smoothed and allowed to dry, and was afterwards coated with starch to give a smooth white surface. The Aztec kept careful records of their history, legends, and laws, and also of the tributes, which conquered people had to pay. Very often paper was one of the items to be given as tribute.

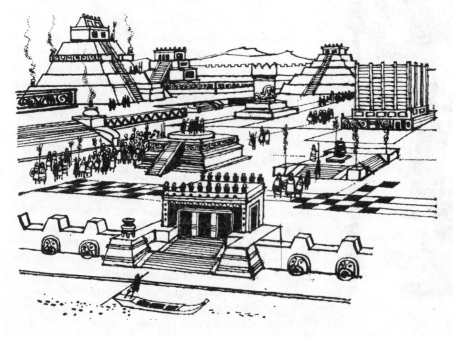

The great Aztec city of Tenochtitlán. This drawing shows how it might have looked in A.D. 1519 when the Spaniards arrived.

The legal system

The Aztec used much of the tribute they received to provide for an excellent system of justice. Each district in the Empire had its own court which tried minor cases. Judges in these courts were elected by the people. All important cases, however, were tried in the high courts in Tenochtitlán, and especially serious cases might be tried by the Emperor himself, in the Supreme Court. In the picture below, drawn by an Aztec artist and preserved in one of their books, you can see three judges condemning a criminal.

Except for local judges, all judges were chosen by the Emperor from among the best graduates of the *calmecac*. They were usually nobles' sons. As payment for their services they were given a house and land by the Emperor, as well as some of the tribute and food from the Imperial storehouses. They could not try cases in which their own relatives or friends were involved, and if they gave an unjust sentence as a result of partiality to one side, they could be put to death.

Court started at eight in the morning and continued throughout the day. The accused and the witnesses were heard only by the judge, as there was neither a jury nor any lawyers. Witnesses gave evidence under oath, and perjury (lying), was punishable by death. The most serious oath a man could take was to call on the name of a great god, and then touch his finger to the ground and then to his lips. If a witness took such an oath, the judge assumed he was telling the truth.

Everyday life and work

The basic unit of Aztec society was the family. Each family had its own area of land it farmed, and a cluster of families formed a clan. There were twenty clans in all. Each clan had its own council and an elected leader. The four wisest of these leaders formed a body, the *tlatoani*, which elected the Emperor. The Emperor was usually elected from among the brothers of the previous ruler, or if there were none, from among the dead Emperor's nephews. As Aztec civilisation developed, new classes of people appeared. Among these were craftsmen – weavers, potters, goldsmiths and

The flywheel. Men, dressed as birds, spun round the centre pole to give an impression of flight. This game was part of a religious festival.

Aztec justice. The three judges have condemned a criminal. Here they witness his execution by garotting.

39

featherworkers – and merchants (*pochteca*). There were also the much less privileged *tlamana*, or slaves. As the Aztec had no pack animals, all burdens had to be carried by the *tlamana*, who sometimes carried loads as heavy as a hundredweight for three or four hundred miles.

Some of these slaves were taken from among the conquered peoples. Some were Aztecs who had been in slavery for debt or crimes against the State. However, they were not cruelly treated. They could marry, and their children were free. They could also own slaves themselves. Furthermore, if they could pay as much as they were bought for, they could buy their freedom. And any slave who ran away and managed to gain entrance to the Emperor's palace gained his freedom.

The *pochteca*, like the *ppolms* of the Maya, occupied a very special place in society. They had their own gods, and their own customs and laws, and lived in their own districts. Like the Maya *ppolms* they enjoyed special privileges and they were not required to serve in the army, or to give any public service in road building or working in the state fields. However, they gave service in another way; in their travels throughout Mexico they frequently acted as spies for the Emperor, and the army depended upon their information before attacking an enemy town. More important than that, the *pochteca* supplied the people of Tenochtitlán with all manner of goods which were sold in the great market at Tlatelolco. They brought cacao, lime and rubber from the tropical regions, and *quetzal* feathers for the Emperor's and warriors' head-dresses, from the jungles.

The market, like the *pochteca*, had its own laws and its own police. All goods had a fixed price and a fixed place in the market. Any vendor who cheated, or was suspected of selling stolen goods was arrested. If he was found guilty, he was sentenced to death. Anyone caught stealing in the marketplace might be clubbed to death by the market police.

Like the Maya, in place of money the Aztecs used quills of gold dust, or crescent-shaped knives of thin beaten copper, or even cacao beans.

At one time or another all classes of Aztec men and women might be seen in the market. The women would be wearing a long skirt held around their hips with a narrow belt, and over it a sleeveless garment called a *huipilli*. Men would wear a loincloth or *maxtli*, and over this a mantle knotted at one shoulder. In cold weather they would wear sandals made of maguey fibre, or of leather, if they were rich. Although both rich and poor wore the same styles, the clothing of the rich was more brightly ornamented with embroidery. In addition, both men and women of the richer classes wore jewellery of copper and gold and especially jade. The men wore earplugs in their earlobes, and women often wore an ornament suspended from a slit in their lower lip. Sometimes they even painted their bodies with different colours – red, blue, yellow, green, or black.

The Aztec woman, like her Mayan sisters, was trained from childhood to undertake adult responsibilities. These consisted mainly of caring for the children and doing household tasks. Girls were usually married at sixteen, while boys were not considered ready for marriage until they reached twenty.

Like the Maya woman, the Aztec housewife spent a good deal of time preparing the family meal. This consisted usually of tortilla, a corn cake served with a sauce called *guacamole*, a thick mixture of tomato, avocado pear and chili peppers. With this was drunk beer, and, very occasionally, cocoa which was a great luxury as it had to be brought by traders from the lowlands.

Because Aztec society was warlike, men were frequently killed in battle or died of wounds. Hence there were more women than men. As a result, in order to ensure that most women married, a system called polygamy (sometimes called polygyny) was permitted. Under this system a man was allowed more than one wife (but a wife could have only one husband). However, though a man might have several wives, the status of the wives varied considerably. One wife, in particular, had well-recognised rights. She was called the First Wife, and gave orders to all the other wives who had to obey. Only the First Wife's children had the right to inherit the father's possessions when he died. Although in theory a man was allowed several wives, in fact it was only among the nobles – men of wealth and influence – that this practice existed. Most families consisted of one man, his wife and children.

Unlike Maya women, who were frequently mistreated by the men in the family, and who were considered as having no rights, Aztec women were assured certain rights and privileges. True, these were not as great as those granted to men, but nonetheless they did offer the women some protection and a guarantee of some measure of respect. For example, it was possible for an Aztec wife to get a divorce under certain circumstances. In fact, both husband and wife could get divorces, although for very different reasons. It is interesting to compare these reasons.

A woman could obtain a divorce if her husband failed to support her, or to educate her children, or if he physically abused her. A man, on the other hand could divorce his wife if she was unable to have children, or was frequently ill-tempered, or if she neglected her household duties. Both men and women could remarry after divorce.

In addition to this kind of protection in marriage, the Aztec woman had certain other rights: she could own property and enter into contracts, in contrast to the Maya woman who could not even inherit her husband's property. If the Aztec woman felt she had been unjustly treated in any matter she could go to court to have her case heard.

There were even cases where Aztec women enjoyed considerable power and prestige beyond their family. For example, many of the most important Aztec deities were female and were served by priestesses who were accorded great respect. It was even possible for an Aztec woman to wield a certain amount of political power. For example, if a boy king were too young to rule, his mother might rule in his stead until he was old enough to take over.

Most Aztecs lived in simple thatched and wattled houses of one room, but the *pochteca*, and *tlatoani*, and other high officials and wealthy people, lived in houses made of stone with a flat roof made from cross beams and tightly plastered. There were no windows, and even the homes of the rich had usually only two rooms. The back room was used for cooking, and was usually open. Sometimes, however, a very wealthy family might have a home of several rooms all built around a central courtyard.

We can see that the Aztecs the Spaniards found

Aztec clothing. Do you think this man and woman are rich or poor?

were in many ways a highly civilised people. In some ways they were even more advanced than the Spaniards of that day. They provided free compulsory education for both boys and girls; they provided for the needs of the people in time of want; their system of justice was honest; their city was cleaner than most European cities of that time; they had discovered a system of mechanics which enabled them to build towering pyramids, using no tools except stone hammers and chisels, and rope dipped in sand to cut through the huge stone blocks. In one hundred years they had developed from a simple tribe to a proud and mighty nation. But in 1519 the Spaniards came. And by 1521, in spite of heroic resistance, the Aztec were themselves conquered, and their civilisation died.

Things to do and think about

1 What do you understand by the word 'civilised'? In what ways do you think the Aztec showed themselves to be civilised?

2 Use an encyclopaedia and look up information about religious beliefs. Do you find any which are similar to those of the Aztec?

3 Compare the Aztec system of government, justice and of education with ours.

4 Choose any event in the life of the Aztec which interests you and either write a story or play about it, or write an imaginary account as if you had been there, or draw a picture of it.

5 Compare Aztec writing with Maya and Egyptian writing. Why is this system of writing called hieroglyphic?

6 Find out what you can about European merchants during the Middle Ages. See how they compare with the Aztec and Maya merchants.

7 Get your art teacher to help you draw some Aztec designs during your art classes.

8 Read carefully the section on women in Aztec society and put into your own words how the Aztec felt about women.

9 Discuss how women are treated in Caribbean society. In what ways do Caribbean couples live together? What do you understand by divorce in Caribbean society today? Outline some of the reasons why couples separate in the Caribbean. How, in your view, does the treatment of women differ today in the Caribbean. Compare your conclusions with what you have read about women's treatment at the time of the Maya.

10 Various aspects of Aztec life are represented in the illustration below. Who do the people represent? Describe their work or life, and the part they played in Aztec society.

These drawings of various economic activities are based on drawings from an old Aztec manuscript.

CHAPTER EIGHT

The Inca

When Pizarro arrived in South America in 1523, the Inca Empire extended from Quito in Ecuador through Peru to almost the south of modern Chile, a distance of four thousand kilometres, and

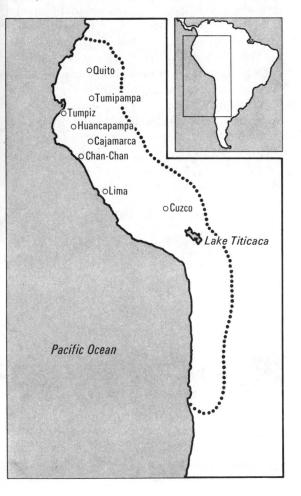

The Land of the Incas.

included parts of Bolivia and Argentina. There were about three and a half million people in this kingdom.

The Inca, however, were only the last of a number of tribes to settle in this region. We have evidence that people were living on the Pacific coast as early as 4000 B.C., and that people were living in the Andes mountains by 1200 B.C.. We know this because of the pottery, tools, objects in graves, and buildings that have been found. One of these buildings has walls which are fifteen metres high today, and were probably even higher when it was first built thousands of years ago. Later, about A.D. 1000, a people called the *Chimu* settled on the Pacific coast, and developed a powerful kingdom. Their capital city covered ten square kilometres, and its inhabitants were supplied with fresh water from a stone reservoir. Using irrigation from distant mountain streams, they irrigated their fields, and to worship their gods they built great stone temples which still stand today.

While the Chimu were building up their civilisation in the coastal valleys, a small tribe in the Andes was conquering its neighbours and making itself very powerful. The name of this tribe was the Inca.

After conquering neighbouring tribes in the mountains, the Inca set up an Empire with its capital at *Cuzco*, high in the Andes. From there, their ruler, whom they called the Lord Inca, governed his vast territory. His armies conquered more and more tribes, and as each tribe was conquered the Lord Inca insisted that the people adopt his own language and religion, and accept Inca government.

The Lord Inca was not only the ruler of an Empire, but the descendant of the Sun itself. Or so his people believed. They worshipped him as a god. Few people were allowed to see him face to face, but had to speak to him from behind a screen. When he travelled he was carried on a litter, for a god's feet must not touch the ground, and when he had finished his meal any food left on his gold and silver plates was burnt in a great ceremony, for no one might touch what had belonged to the great Lord Inca.

Government and taxation

Below the Lord Inca were the nobles, who were all members of the royal family. They were the governors of the provinces which the Inca armies captured. A group of officials called *curacas*, assisted these governors, and were responsible for a hundred taxpayers in each district. Under the *curacas* were foremen responsible for ten taxpayers. It was important for the Inca people to be carefully organised in this way, for, as we shall soon see, the people paid their taxes or *mita*, in the form of national service, and the Lord Inca needed to know how much service was due from each person.

The *mita* took many forms, and all the Inca's subjects except the nobles were required to give it. Sometimes it took the form of work in the government-owned gold and silver mines. Sometimes it consisted of working on roads and bridges and the construction of public buildings like temples and fortresses. Certain regions of the empire had specialised forms of *mita*. For example, one province provided all the dancers for the Lord Inca's court as its *mita*; another was required to supply the carved and scented wood used for the ceremonial fires. Still another province had to provide the specially trained runners who carried messages throughout the empire, and constituted the Inca postal service. Yet another region supplied the Emperor's litter bearers and most people, as we have already seen, paid their *mita* in the form of army or agricultural service. All the Inca's subjects in this way contributed to the running of the government. Even the priests contributed through their prayers, and the goldsmiths in making the splendid gold ornaments, although these were not considered to be *mita*.

Because the Inca Empire was so large, and because it was necessary to keep a close check on the various activities that were taking place, there were a great many officials, all of whom were appointed by the Emperor. The priests were considered to be civil servants and were appointed in the same way as the judges and the many officials who saw to the distribution of food from the government storehouses, which we read about in Chapter 4. One of the most important of all these officials was the *Quipucamayoc*, or *Keeper of the Quipu*.

The *quipu* was a device invented by the Inca for reckoning numbers. Unlike the Maya and the Aztec they had no written language or numerals. Instead they relied on a system of knots and coloured cords of different lengths and thicknesses to enable them to calculate. Each district and province and *ayllu* (clan) was represented by a different colour, or cord of a different thickness. By means of the size and placing of the knots on these cords, the Lord Inca was able to check on the number of able-bodied men in his empire, and on the amount of *mita* which each man and each *ayllu* owed, as well as how much *mita* had already been served. The *quipu* also enabled him to check on how much grain had been stored in the royal granaries, and how many pounds of llama wool had been collected, and how much gold and silver

Important Inca officials were carried in litters.

44

Inca reckoning was done on a quipu. Quipu means 'knot'. Can you think how the Inca used the knots as a counting system?

had been mined and put in the Inca's treasury. All these *quipu* records were kept in special offices in Cuzco.

As the Inca armies conquered more and more territory and the population of the empire grew, the government in Cuzco took measures to see that the newly conquered people were loyal to the Lord Inca. The sons and daughters of their leaders were taken as hostages to Cuzco where they were educated in the same way as the children of Inca nobles, and were taught to be loyal to the Lord Inca. The rest of the people were removed from their district and settled in another part of the empire among loyal subjects, so that they could not cause a rebellion. However, the places where they were resettled were as much as possible like their original homelands, and in order to help them to settle easily, the officials were ordered to supply them with food, clothing, and tools if necessary. An Inca noble was appointed as Governor, and he immediately ordered that a Temple of the Sun be built, in honour of the Lord Inca. Although the conquered people were treated kindly, they were forced to adopt certain Inca customs. They had to speak the Inca language, *Quechua*, and to wear Inca clothing. However, they were also made to wear their own distinctive head-dress, so that they could be easily identified.

Everyday life and work

Let us see what everyday life was like among the people living in the Inca empire. We would notice at once that there were no really poor people. Only the Emperor was rich, but everyone had enough to eat and to wear. Houses were very simple. Usually they consisted of only one room with a thatched roof. There were no windows, and very little furniture. Everyone, including the Lord Inca, slept on the floor on hides, or woollen mats, but although the homes of the commoners were bare, the Inca's palace was decorated with solid gold and silver ornaments hanging on the walls. In all homes a fire was kept burning to keep it warm in the high Andes, but wood was scarce, and llama and alpaca dung was often used as fuel.

Everyone ate twice a day, with the main meal at about our breakfast time. The staple food varied according to whether the family lived in the lowlands or the mountains. Corn was the main

The interior of an Inca house.

food of the lowland people, who ground it in a mill and then cooked it into porridge. In the highlands, people depended on potato, which they preserved by freezing and then thawing it out and squeezing out the liquid, after which they allowed the potato to dry. Dry potato, or *chunu*, was often eaten with dried and pounded strips of meat called *charqui*, which were taken from guinea pigs. Most food was either boiled or roasted, and was flavoured with salt which the people licked from their hand, instead of cooking it with the food.

Except that head-dresses varied from province to province, the Inca people dressed very much alike. Even the Emperor and nobles wore the same style garments as the commoners, although they were made of much finer cloth. The higher classes also wore a great deal of jewelry, especially large golden ear plugs. The right to wear these ear plugs was a sign of the Emperor's favour, and was greatly prized.

Inca garments were never tailored to fit, but consisted of one piece of cloth which was pinned at the shoulder. Sandals of untanned llama hide were worn. The special mark of the Emperor was a four-inch wide fringe which he wore around his head. This was made of small gold tubes from which red tassels hung. His garments were specially woven by priestesses who were carefully selected for this duty from the age of about ten years, and specially trained.

For women in Inca society, life was similar to that of women in other Amerindian cultures. With a few exceptions, which we shall read about shortly, all Inca were expected to marry. Girls were betrothed shortly after puberty which was marked by special rites. At the first sign of menstruation all her relatives were invited to a special ceremony which was held in the girl's home. The young girl was required to fast for three days, at the end of which time her mother washed her, dressed her in special clothes and white sandals, and presented her to the relatives. One of her uncles then gave her the name which she would use for the rest of her life – names like Egg, Pure, Star and Gold were common. Following the rites, the girls would join other boys and girls of her age in the public square where they would be paired off (though they were allowed

some say in the choice of partner). The pairs were then married in a ceremony by a public official. This ceremony was not a religious one as we understand the word today. However, the Inca did not make the same distinctions as we do between religion and everyday life. The wedding ceremony, which was an important event in Inca society, was an aspect of the religious life of the people. After the wedding there was great feasting and rejoicing, after which the young couple started their new life as adult members of the community.

Since children began working with their parents from as young as five years old, both husband and wife were accustomed to the hard work that adult life entailed. We have seen the importance of agriculture in Inca economy, and it should not surprise us to learn that among the Inca, as in other cultures, a large part of the agricultural labour was performed by the women. In addition, women bore all responsibility for their children and households. A major part of the Inca woman's time was spent in carding and spinning yarn, then weaving it into cloth for her families' garments.

Despite the fact that men and women worked equally hard, the Inca did not regard them as of equal value. We recall that there was no private property among the Inca; all land was controlled by the *ayallu* to which everyone belonged, and was then allotted by the *ayallu* to each family. The way in which this land was allotted reflects the lesser regard in which Inca society held women. When a couple married they were allotted a *topo* (about an acre) of land to cultivate for their own needs. At the birth of a son, the couple received an additional *topo*. But at the birth of a daughter, they were granted only a half-*topo*. Moreover, when a son married, he retained his half *topo* of land. When a daughter married, however, her half *topo* reverted to the common lands. In other words, while the husband brought valuable land to the marriage, the wife came with nothing, an indication of her lesser status.

Most Inca families consisted of a husband, his wife and children. However, as was true in other warlike societies, such as the Aztec for instance, the system of polygamy was permitted. Among the Inca as among the Aztec, this was the case only among the nobles and the wealthy. In such a case there was only one 'Real Wife' (like the Aztecs' 'First Wife'). She ruled over the other wives or concubines in the household and could not be divorced. If the Real Wife died, a man could take another to replace her, but he could not elevate one of his secondary wives to that position.

The everyday life of most Inca women was similar to that of women in other Amerindian societies; their main responsibilities lay in looking after households and children and in assisting in the production of food. However, as the climate in which most of the Inca lived was much colder than that of the lowlands which other groups inhabited, the production of blankets and clothing for warmth was a necessity. The preparation of yarn, and weaving of cloth was an activity in which Inca women excelled. Pieces of Inca garments and other textiles have been found which are unequalled anywhere in the world in the fineness of their weave and the beauty of their colours. Caring for the animals which produced the required wool; cleaning and spinning the wool into yarn; preparing dyes for the yarn, and then weaving the unbelievably intricate patterns took up a great deal of women's time. So important was the weaving of beautiful textiles that it was one of the skills for which a group known as 'Chosen Women' were especially trained.

Thus, Inca women participated in society in a number of different ways. Unfortunately, there is still a lot we do not really understand about Inca society and there is still a lot to learn. We do know, however, that there was a special group of women called 'Chosen Women'. Every year, a government official visited each village throughout the land and examined all those girls who had reached the age of ten. Those whom he felt were the most beautiful and physically perfect were removed from their villages and sent to special schools. There they remained for four years. During that time they were taught the mysteries of the Inca religion, the art of weaving the fine textiles worn by the priests and priestesses, and the brewing of a special beer called *chicha*, used in religious ceremonies. When their training was completed, there was a further choice. Some of these girls were given to the nobles, or even to the Emperor as second wives. Others, called *mammacuna*, were honoured by being made priestesses serving the Sun God. These did not marry but lived in houses attached to Temples of the Sun. There they assisted in religious ceremonies, and, because they were priestesses to the Sun, were accorded great respect.

Religion

Priests and priestesses played an important part in the life of the Inca people, for the Inca religion like that of the Maya and Aztec, required many ceremonies and sacrifices. Some of these took place daily. Every morning, for instance, the priests lit the sacred fire, and threw food into it as they recited the following prayer:

'Eat this, Lord Sun, and acknowledge thy children'

In the evening a red llama was sacrificed. During the day the priests were busy caring for the sacred objects of gold and silver in the temples, hearing confessions, and setting penances for those who confessed their sins. They also specialised in medicine and often performed operations of a very high standard.

The greatest of Inca gods was *Viracocha*, who was the creator of all gods. Other important gods were *Inti*, the Sun God, *Mama-kilya*, the Moon Mother, and *Illapa* the God of Thunder, who controlled rain.

All these gods influenced the *huacas*, or sacred places, which we read about in Chapter 4. These *huacas* were to be found everywhere. All snow-capped mountains were *huacas*, and so were dangerous spots on the road. At these spots travellers stopped to make their prayers and left a stone, or a handful of straw. The Inca also built great stone temples to their gods.

Inca temples were not built on pyramids, however, but consisted of one large room with a curved wall, and thatched roof. The *Coriancha*, or Temple of the Sun, in Cuzco was the largest of these. Although they used no mortar, the Inca masons fitted the stones together so perfectly that even today it is impossible to fit even a thin blade between them. Inside the temple were gold idols and the bodies of dead Emperors.

Communications

Inca engineering skill was shown in many ways, but especially in their building of roads and bridges. Because of the extent of the empire, it was essential to have quick means of transportation, and because of the varied topography of the empire engineers had to overcome many natural obstacles. Fortunately, because the Inca, like the Maya and Aztec, had no wheeled vehicles, their roads and bridges did not have to be very wide, or to carry much weight.

Wherever possible the Inca built straight roads, usually 1 metre wide, but often, because of the mountainous terrain, the roads had to zigzag around a mountainside. Sometimes the slope was so steep that the engineers cut steps instead of attempting to build roads. Their greatest skill, however, was shown in the building of bridges to cross the many ravines which crossed the mountain ranges. The most skilfully constructed of these bridges were the swinging bridges over the deep gorges. These were made of fibre cables twisted to form a rope as much as forty centimetres in diameter, which were anchored at both ends by being deeply buried in the earth. Towers were built at both ends of the gorge to hold down the ropes, and thinner cables were attached to these towers to form hand-rails. The cross-sticks were laid over the cables and these covered with mats or mud to make walking over easier. The bridges swayed dizzily in the breeze, but the pedestrians and llama packs which crossed them were quite safe, for it was an important part of the *mita* to keep the bridges in repair. Damaging or destroying bridges was treason and punished by death.

But almost the only people to use these bridges and roads were those travelling on official business, for Inca subjects were not allowed to travel far from their homes. However, at any time one could see the Emperor's runners carrying messages along the flat roads of the coastal plain, or across the dizzying mountain bridges. They might be carrying the all-important *quipu*, or messages regarding an attempted revolt in a distant province, or even fish from the Pacific to the Emperor at Cuzco. These young men were trained to run at great speeds. Fresh fish could be brought from the sea to Cuzco in two days by runners.

The runners' *mita* was very carefully organised, for it was one of the most important. The young men served for fifteen days at a time, during which period they were on duty twenty-four hours a day. They worked in pairs, staying in small shelters built about a mile apart. One runner of each pair kept a look-out for an approaching messenger, and ran out to meet him. As they ran on together for a short distance, he was given the message, seized the *quipu*, and ran swiftly the mile to the next shelter where he in turn was relieved by a fresh runner. These runners ensured that the Emperor in Cuzco was kept informed of all events within the empire, and that the Inca government was efficiently run.

The legal system

As among the Inca and Aztec, justice was quick and honest, and a noble who broke the law was punished more severely than a commoner. The Inca judges took special circumstances into account when they were delivering sentence. For instance, if a man could show that he robbed because of want, he was punished less severely. But the official who had allowed him to suffer such want was very harshly punished. Planning revolt, destroying government property, or robbing the state granaries, were all crimes punishable by death. But there was little crime in the Inca empire, because the peoples' wants were provided for. There was no unemployment, and no hunger. Nor was there any freedom. The Lord Inca ruled his people as their king and as their god, and all power belonged to him.

In the reign of the Lord Inca, *Atuallpa*, the Spaniard Pizarro appeared. Like the Aztec, the Inca people thought he was a god returning as their legends had foretold. When they discovered that Pizarro and his men were not gods, but greedy and treacherous men, it was too late. Atuallpa was murdered, and the mighty Inca empire crumbled to the dust.

Things to do and think about

1 Would you have liked to live as a commoner in the Inca empire?

Many journeys would have been impossible without bridging the deep gorges.

2 Pretend you were an Inca boy or girl and write an imaginary account of your father's or older brother's *mita*.

3 What evidence is there in this chapter that the Inca valued gold and silver?

4 What do you think of Inca laws and justice? How do they compare with those in your country?

5 What group of people have we not heard about among the Inca, who were very important among the Aztec and Maya? Can you think of any reasons why these people would not be important in the Inca empire?

6 Find out what is meant by *feudal* and *totalitarian* government. Which of these words describes Inca government? Find out what service in medieval Europe was similar to the *mita*.

7 Whom would you consider more tolerant of other people, the Inca or the Maya? Why?

8 Look carefully at the illustration above. What are the four large white structures? What aspects of Inca life are conveyed in this illustration? What might be contained in the baskets that are being carried?

9 What is the difference between being *important* and being *respected*? Consider the role of women in the three Amerindian societies you have read about and say whether you think the women were important and respected in these societies.

CHAPTER NINE

The Arawaks

The first people to see the Spaniards' arrival in the New World were a brown-skinned people we call the *Arawaks*. Fishermen, cultivators clearing land, boys snaring birds, all gazed with wonder at the strange ships whose great square sails resembled the wings of some enormous bird. Also watching was the grave and stately *cacique*, whose crown of green, white, and red stones, and whose feathered cape, showed him to be their leader.

These people were of middle height, plump in build, and had straight black hair which they usually wore long, and often decorated with parrot feathers. Their foreheads were flat and sloping, for like the Maya, mothers bound their babies' heads between two boards. All wondered about the tall, fair-skinned strangers, curious to know who they were, and what they wanted from the inhabitants of these tiny tropical islands.

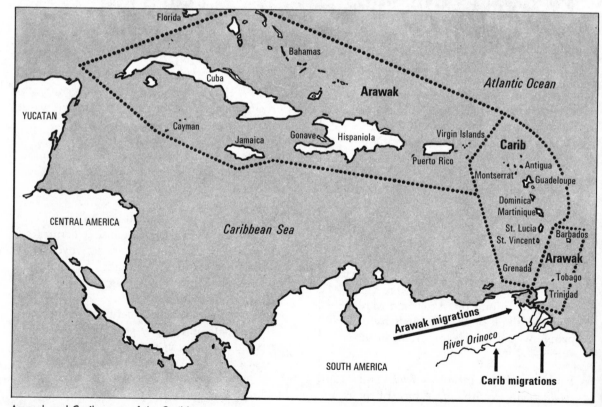

Arawak and Carib areas of the Caribbean.

For over fourteen hundred years the Indians had inhabited the mountainous and fertile islands of the Caribbean. At about the time of Jesus' birth they had left their original homes in the Orinoco valley and had sailed up the Antilles, leaving groups to settle on each island in turn. There they lived in relative security, though they had always to face the threat of drought, hurricanes and sudden Carib raids.

When we speak of the Arawaks, however, we must remember that they were not a single people living in one place like the Maya, Aztec and Inca. When the Arawaks migrated northward from South America they settled in separate groups on the various islands. Most settled in the Greater Antilles – Hispaniola, Cuba, Puerto Rico and Jamaica. A much smaller number settled in the Lesser Antilles. Since these settlements were widely separated, communication between them was difficult, so it is not surprising that there were differences between the various Arawak communities, just as there are between various Caribbean communities today. Nevertheless, all Arawak societies shared some characteristics.

The Arawaks were primarily an agricultural people, so their scattered villages were usually built on fertile land. Since fishing was also an important part of their economy, these villages were often built near the sea, either on the plains, or on hillsides overlooking the sea. Some of these villages were quite large, numbering as many as 3,000 inhabitants, though most were much smaller with perhaps a few hundred inhabitants or even less. They were well planned, usually circular in shape, with a ball court or ceremonial plaza as their central feature. This plaza was often surrounded by earthen or stone embankments from which spectators could watch the ball games. These games were one aspect of the religious ceremonies which played such a great part in the life of the Arawaks. The chief's house, was built next to the plaza. Not only was each village well planned, but Arawak settlements as a whole were highly organised. The larger islands, for example were divided into provinces, with several villages in each province. Each village was ruled by a headman, while the province was ruled by the *cacique*. For most Arawak people, however, it was the headman's power which mattered. He was the one who organised the work of the village, deciding when land should be prepared, crops planted and harvested, and any surplus stored for distribution in the community. All work was done communally, the commoners and slaves doing the work which the nobles supervised. The headman was also the religious leader of his village, and the judge whose word was law and who could sentence people to death for disobedience. In fact, however, there seems to have been very few laws as we know them. The one serious crime appears to have been theft, for which the culprit was put to death by impalement. This was a particularly gruesome and painful method in which an individual was pierced through with a pointed stake and left to die slowly.

The cacique – leader of the community

When we speak of the *cacique* among the Arawak we have to remember that he had two roles. In his own village he was the headman and had the power of any other headman. However, in addition, the *cacique* ruled over the whole province and could give orders that affected people living in all the villages in that province. For example, he was the one who, after consulting with the nobles or *mitaynos*, decided whether the people of a certain island would go to war against a neigh-

A duho – the cacique's ceremonial stool.

51

bouring island or against another province. He could levy a kind of tax on the people of his province. This might be in the form of agricultural produce, or of weapons. Or he might demand that a certain number of men be sent from villages to take part in the raids. As was true for all rulers in Arawak society, he was all-powerful and his orders had to be obeyed on pain of death.

Like the *halach uinich* of the Maya, the *cacique* inherited his position. Unlike the Maya, however, the Arawak recognised matrilineal descent, that is, inheritance through the mother's family. Moreover, the *cacique* might be a woman. It did not often happen, but if no suitable man were available, it was possible for a woman to inherit the position of *cacique* and to have the power that went with it. Nobles, or *mitaynos*, also inherited their position, while people born commoners remained in that class. Slaves were usually men and women captured in wars; female captives were given to outstanding warriors as concubines. We can see, then, that Arawak society had a strong class structure. In societies which have such class divisions, the most important person enjoys certain privileges as well as power, and this was certainly true for the *cacique* and his family.

Because of his importance, the *cacique* had many privileges. As with other Indians of the Americas, he was given part of the harvest for himself and his family. Special cassava cakes were made for him. His house, or *bohio*, was built by the village men, and was larger than that of the others though, like theirs, it was of wattle with a thatch roof. The *cacique* and his family wore ornaments of gold and copper alloy called *guanin*, for gold was a sign of rank among them, and his wives' skirts were longer than those of the other women, for length of skirt was also a mark of high rank. His canoe, made by the village men, was the largest in the village, and the only one to be painted, and when he travelled by land, he was carried in a litter, while his son was carried on servants' shoulders. At his death, the *cacique* was either burnt in his own hut or buried in a cave or a grave. If buried in a grave, a mound was built to mark the spot. As with many tribes at this level of development, the Arawaks also buried two or more of the favourite wives of the *cacique* with him. They were provided with a calabash of water and a portion of cassava.

This was to help feed them on their journey to *Coyaba*, where they would continue to serve their husband.

Gods and spirit worship

The Arawak *zemis* were idols made of many different kinds of material – wood, bone, stone, or even cotton – which were felt to contain the forces of nature or the spirits of the ancestors. Each family had its own *zemi* which it prized highly, and some families kept the bones of dead ancestors in a basket for use as *zemis*. The *cacique*'s *zemis* were felt to be more powerful than anyone else's and this was one way in which he held his power, for the people felt that the *zemis* controlled everything – sickness, weather, crops, even peace and war – and that only the *cacique* and other priests could speak with them.

Even though the ordinary people could not converse with the *zemis*, each home had its own *zemi* in a place of honour on a small table. A bowl of snuff (*cahoba*) or powdered tobacco, was placed before it, and when the person wished to pray he placed the *cahoba* on the *zemi*'s flat-topped head, and inhaled from it, through his nostrils, from a Y-shaped cane tube. He often rubbed the *zemi* with

A cotton zemi.

52

assava to feed it, for the Arawaks felt that if their *zemi* went hungry they themselves would fall ill.

Because they depended upon the *zemis'* advice before taking important decisions, the Arawaks laid much importance on religious ceremonies. The *cacique* announced the day on which a ceremony was to take place, and when the conch shell was blown all the people assembled, wearing their finery. Their bodies were carefully washed, and were painted red and white and black. The men wore their feathered cloaks, and the women decorated their arms and legs with shells and coral.

When all were assembled, the entire people formed a procession, with the *cacique* at its head, playing a wooden gong. He led them to the sacred hut on the outskirts of the village, and there he and the priests entered to pray. First they tickled their throats with swallow-sticks to make themselves vomit, and so prove to the *zemis* that no impurity remained within them. After this they each smoked the smouldering *cahoba*, drawing deep breaths until they lost consciousness. It was then that the *zemis* were supposed to speak to them.

The Arawaks believed in many gods, whom the *zemis* represented. The most important of these were the God of the Sky and the Goddess of the Earth, from whom all living things had descended. They had a legend to explain the creation of man, which told how in the beginning all humans, and the sun, were kept in a cave and let out only occasionally. One day, however, the guardian of the cave forgot to close the opening and they all escaped. The men and women went to different islands, and for his carelessness the guardian was turned into a stone. In addition to the gods of sky and earth, the Arawaks believed in a God of the Moon, which they thought was the sun's twin brother. They also believed in spirits called *opia*, which belonged to the dead, and who returned at night to try to enter their bodies. For this reason they ventured out at night only in groups, and protected themselves by wearing *zemis* round their necks or on their foreheads.

Festivals, games and everyday life

Many festivals marked the Arawak year, some religious and some not. For example, the naming of a baby was a time of rejoicing, for the Arawaks felt a child without a name would meet with great misfortune. The wedding of a *cacique*, and the inauguration of a new *cacique* were times of festivity. So was harvest time, or the return of a victorious war party. During these festivities the emphasis was on dancing and singing to the music of drums, reed pipes and wooden gongs.

The everyday activities of the Arawaks centred around providing food and shelter. As we saw in Chapter 4, the women did the planting. They were also responsible for preparing the food. Since the main food of the Arawaks was cassava, which is poisonous in its natural state, preparing it required very great care. First the root was grated on a board covered with small pebbles or rough coral until it formed a paste. This was put into a wicker tube, one end of which was hung from a branch, while a weight was attached to the other end. This caused the tube to contract, and forced the poisonous liquid out through the wicker. The paste which remained was left to dry and then pounded into flour using a stone mortar and pestle. The flour was formed into flat cakes and baked on a clay griddle until the cakes were hard and dry. In this way they could keep for some time. In some islands, in addition to cassava cakes

The cacique's house — his bohio.

53

the women made a kind of corn bread with green corn whose kernels they crushed. But the tastiest dish of all was *pepperpot*.

While the women were busy with their other work, the pepperpot was left to simmer on the fire. Into a large clay pot were put cassava juice, from which the poison had been extracted, and beans, peanuts, potato, and some meat – perhaps iguana, or turtle, or yellow snake – and pepper. The family was fed three times a day, and as some pepperpot was removed more ingredients were added so that the delicious soup was already ready. As a change, the family might be given meat or fish, which had been smoked for about twelve hours over a slow fire to preserve it. This might be served with *cassareep*, a sauce of cassava juice, salt and pepper. Pineapple, guava, mammee apple, and star apple added to the meal, and sometimes a kind of beer was drunk.

While the food was slowly cooking, the girls and women might be busy spinning and weaving cotton cloth, especially in Jamaica, where cotton grew in great abundance. Hammocks were made of cotton-string which was then netted together. The women wore thin cotton bands on their arms and legs, and those that were married wore a loincloth. Ears, noses, and often the lower lip were pierced so that ornaments – usually gold – could be worn. Bodies of both men and women were painted, specially on ceremonial occasions. The hair was usually worn loose and flowing, although the Arawaks of the Bahamas cut theirs in a fringe.

We have seen that to some extent an Arawak woman might enjoy prestige and power among the Arawaks, if she happened to inherit the position of *cacique*. However, this would have been extremely rare and for most women life seems to have been the same as in the other societies we have looked at. Columbus remarked that Arawak women seemed to do most of the work, and from what we have read of other Amerindian societies that should come as no surprise. One tantalizing hint of something different comes from the report of some Spanish soldiers that they saw women warriors on the island of St Croix. How they were chosen, how they were treated, and what their position in society was we do not know. We also do not know whether these women really were 'a special case'

or whether, in fact, women warriors were much more common than we have often supposed. But obviously some Arawak women, in some places were able to act in non traditional ways. For most however, life meant the usual round of labour and subservience.

Meantime, while the women were busy with household activities, the men were also going about their share of the work. In Chapter 3 we learnt something of how they caught fish and meat for the family. In addition to this, they had to make the canoes from which they fished, and to build their own and the *cacique*'s home, as well as making all their stone tools. Canoes were dug out and shaped from large cedar or silk cotton trees. To our eyes they would have looked quite awkward because they were square at both ends. Some of these canoes might have been as long as 20 metres, and the Arawaks could travel great distances in them, paddling from island to island to barter goods since they do not seem to have used sails. Manioc, pepper, stools, pottery, carved stone objects, and especially gold were among the things they exchanged. Some places specialised in certain commodities. For example, Hispaniola was renowned for its gold, and Gonave, an island on the west coast of Hispaniola was noted for its woodwork. Trinidadian Arawaks traded extensively with the mainland for gold.

Arawak housing

Making the houses was another of the men's tasks. Some of these were very large, like those in Trinidad, which were bell-shaped, and housed about a hundred people. In all Arawak settlements several families shared one house, which was called a *caneye*. It was round, and made of wattle with a thatched roof. Sometimes it had windows, but not always, and there was almost never a smokehole. However, these houses were very sturdily built especially since they had to withstand hurricanes. Wooden posts were placed firmly in the ground to form a circle about five paces apart and laced together with springy branches and grass. Transverse beams, as shown in the diagram, were tied on the top of the posts, and a pole placed in the centre of the structure. The

54

ntre pole and the transverse beams were then
connected with thin poles, and these were covered
with grass or palm leaves to form a conical roof.
The *cacique's* house (*bohio*) was often larger than
the ordinary *caneye*, and was rectangular in shape.

These Arawak houses were cool, rainproof and
windproof and need never be replaced if they
were well built. Except for the *zemi*, and the
hammocks, and some clay pots which were hung
from the roof out of the reach of ants, there was no
furniture in the Arawak home.

Raiders and warriors

Although the Arawak were primarily farmers,
they were also at times intrepid warriors. Usually
their so-called wars were raids on neighbouring
territories, fought to establish fishing or hunting
rights. Or they might be wars of revenge.

Arawaks went into battle under a noble who
had put himself forward as their leader. Painting
their bodies red, and carrying their round or
square-shaped shields, they fought with spears and
clubs. Winners at times practised cannibalism on
their defeated enemies, but usually captives were
brought home, the men to be slaves, the women to
become concubines.

Despite their own raids, the Arawaks feared
those made on them by the Caribs. They did not
know, when they saw fair-skinned strangers off
their shores, that these would be a much more
dangerous enemy than the Caribs had ever been.

Things to do and think about

1 In some places Arawak drawings can be
   seen in caves. Why do you suppose they
   made drawings there? If you should see
   such a drawing make a copy of it. Those
   of you who live in Guyana should try to
   visit Tumatumamari and see the *timehri*
   (the Arawak symbols used in writing)
   there.

2 Do any people in your country live in
   thatched houses? How are they made?
   Find out in what other parts of the world
   people live in thatched houses today.

3 Make an Arawak pepperpot soup. If
   pepperpot is made in your country,
   describe how it differs from an Arawak
   pepperpot.

4 What do we use cassava or manioc for
   today? What food that we make with
   cassava is similar to Arawak food? Try
   making some the way the Arawaks did.

5 Have you ever slept in a hammock?
   Describe what it is like. Can you think of
   any advantages in using a hammock rather
   than a bed?

6 Where do you suppose the Arawaks got
   the dye for their faces and bodies?

7 What does the term 'barbarian' mean?
   Europeans often described the native
   people they encountered as barbarians.
   Why might the Spanish have considered
   that these people were barbarians? Are
   there aspects of Arawak life and culture
   which lead you to disagree with the
   Spaniards?

A caneye, an Arawak family house. Some caneyes could
house as many as 100 people. They were designed to be
strong enough to withstand a hurricane. Try and design a
house yourself using only natural substances that would be
as strong as a caneye.

CHAPTER TEN

The Caribs

Like the Arawaks, the Caribs originated in South America. Like the Arawaks, too, there were many different tribes of Caribs, who differed in some ways but whose culture was similar enough that we can talk of a Carib culture.

About 1,000 years after the Arawaks had migrated north and settled in the Antilles, some of these Carib people followed suit. By Columbus' time Caribs had taken over northwestern Trinidad and possibly eastern Puerto Rico, and the islands of the Lesser Antilles where they eliminated the earlier Arawak settlers.

The Caribs were always fewer in number than the Arawaks, perhaps because they were primarily a warlike people suffering heavy losses in their many wars. The Arawaks had every reason to fear the Caribs who continually raided their settlements looking for food and slaves.

Daily life

On the shores near their villages, which were built on the windward side of the island to guard against surprise attack, the Caribs posted sentries whose duty it was to warn of any approaching canoes. When warning was given, the Carib men swiftly paddled out in their own canoes to meet the strangers, and to learn their intentions. If they were peaceful, they were escorted to shore with great ceremony, and led immediately to the village *carbet*, or *tabouïi*, which was the men's house, and the most important building. At the *carbet* they were greeted by the captain of the village, and names were exchanged. After this, they were taken to the nearby stream where they were able to wash, and then taken to a clean hut where they were invited to rest on a new *amais*, kind of bed. Meantime, the women hurried to prepare a feast.

The Caribs ate a great quantity of sea food and pepper, but they ate neither salt nor pig nor turtle for they thought these foods would make them stupid. Nor did they eat much fat. Sometimes they made a soup from agouti bones and other leftovers which they seasoned with pepper sauce, cassava flour and oysters; sometimes they ate grilled fish which they cooked slowly on a wooden grid, served with a sauce called *couii*, and eaten with sweet potato and yam. Their favourite dish, however, was a stew made with crab and cassava.

This copy of an old print shows a small carbet. Many carbets were very much larger.

nd seasoned with *taumalin* sauce. This was made with lemon juice, pepper, and the green meat of the crab near the shell. With this they drank a kind of cassava beer called *ouicou*, which was very intoxicating. When the guests had eaten their fill they were entertained with singing and dancing to the music of reed pipes, drums and whistles. The guests were welcome to stay as long as they liked, and, when at last they decided to leave, they were loaded with gifts, and entreated to stay longer.

During this long visit, the Caribs' guests would have had many opportunities to observe how their hosts lived, and what kind of people they were. They would have described the Caribs as a brown-kinned people who flattened their foreheads, and usually went naked, with a loin-cloth for women, decorating their bodies with a dye called *roucou*. This was made from vegetable dye and oil which the Caribs felt toughened their skin and protected them from insect bites. They would have discovered, too, that the Caribs were a clean people, who always built their villages beside a stream so that they could wash daily.

Carib houses were large and rectangular in shape. In addition to hammocks, Caribs sometimes slept on an *amais* which consisted of a piece of cotton folded at both ends and hung from the roof. The hammocks had a small packet of ash placed at each end, which it was thought would make them last longer. Other furniture included stools made from red or yellow wood, highly polished, and a table made from latanier rushes. In every home was found an idol of the family's *maboya*. At night the homes were lighted by candles made of a sweet smelling gum. Outside, the Caribs built a small storehouse in which they kept their warclubs, their household utensils, their stone tools, and extra beds and hammocks.

Many men among the Caribs were maimed, but instead of being pitied, these men were respected, for it was honourable among them to have suffered wounds in battle.

Although the Caribs wore no clothing except a loin cloth, they decorated themselves in many ways. We have read in Chapter 5 of the *caracoli* which the warriors wore. Women wore bracelets, called *rassada*, on their arms and legs, and men sometimes wore necklaces made of their enemies' teeth strung on cotton. Both men and women wore bracelets and necklaces of amber, shell, agouti teeth, seeds, and coral, and bored holes in their lips and ear lobes into which they inserted smooth fishbones and other ornaments. Around their necks, also, were worn small idols representing the powerful and frightening *maboya*, of whom we shall learn shortly. For very special occasions the men wore feathered cloaks and head-dresses of heron or macaw feathers, and at all times they took great care of their long hair which, as with the Arawaks, it was the women's duty to comb and oil daily.

The Carib engaged very little in agriculture. It is even possible that what agriculture they did engage in they had learnt from the Arawak women they captured. The Carib did, on the other hand, produce two very fine articles: hammocks woven from cotton on which they slept, and baskets woven from local materials. These were tightly woven in two layers, with a lining of leaves between the outer and inner layer which made them waterproof. Some of these baskets were so large that when turned upside down with legs attached they were used as tables.

In such a warlike society sons were naturally highly valued. At a son's birth there was a special ceremony during which the father was cut with agouti teeth and expected to bear the pain without flinching so that his son would grow up to be brave. The boy was periodically rubbed with the fat of slaughtered Arawaks so that he might absorb their courage, and then, as we saw in Chapter 5, came the great moment when he underwent the initiation ceremony which changed him from a boy to a man, and a warrior. Now he had a new name, and was a true Carib.

Religion

Most Carib boys were trained as warriors, but a small group were trained for an equally important position, that of priest, or *boyez*. When a boy was to be trained as a *boyez*, he was apprenticed for several years to an older priest. During this time he frequently had to fast, and to abstain from eating meat. Then the boy had to undergo an initiation ceremony as severe as that of a warrior. If he passed through this initiation successfully, his teacher took him to the *carbet* where fruit, cassava and *ouicou* were sacrificed to the priest's *maboya*. The priest sang and smoked, inviting his *maboya* to enter the *carbet*. When at last the *maboya* was thought to have come, the *boyez* asked him to provide a special *maboya* for the apprentice. If the *maboya* agreed, the young man became a fully-fledged *boyez*, with his own personal *maboya* to help him perform his duties.

Since most of the *boyez* duties had to do with overcoming evil spirits, the *maboya* was the most important of the Carib idols. They felt that each person had his own *maboya*, and that all evils, whether sickness, defeat in battle, or even death, came as a result of a spell put on them by an enemy *maboya*. When a person was ill, for instance, the *boyez* was called in to defeat the *maboya's* evil spell. First the house was thoroughly cleaned, and gifts of cassava, *ouicou* and first fruits were laid on a table, or *matoutou*, for the *maboya*. The *matoutou* was placed at one end of the room, and stools for each member of the family were placed at the other end. When it was dark, the *boyez* entered and began his incantations, addressed to the patient's good god, for the Caribs believed that everyone had his own good god, as well as a *maboya*. Then he struck the ground three times with his left foot. Then he put a lighted tobacco into his mouth and blew the smoke upwards four or five times. After this he rubbed a leaf in his hands and scattered the powder on the patient's body. Finally he prescribed a mixture of herbs to be given, and warned the family to take strong revenge against the *maboya* which had caused the sickness.

Unfortunately, the patient often died in spite of the treatment. In that case, the *boyez* explained, a stronger revenge was necessary. Meantime, all the dead man's relatives examined the body to see if he had died by sorcery. After this, the body was carefully washed and painted red, and the hair was combed and oiled. Then it was placed on a stool in a grave dug inside the *carbet*. For ten days, the relatives would bring food and water to the graveside, and build a fire around it so that the corpse would not get cold. After ten days the grave was filled in, and the dead man's possessions burnt. When the grave was completed, there was dancing over it, and as a sign of mourning the relatives cut their hair. Later, a feast was held ov the grave, and often the dead man's hou especially if he was a chief, was burnt down.

Perhaps more people would have survived the Carib had had more respect for the knowled of healing that their women possessed. As was tr in many societies, Carib women had a special a very practical knowledge of natural sources healing. They knew which herbs or roots or plar would cure indigestion, or counteract poison, relieve allergies. Unfortunately, however, it w not these women healers whom Caribs feared, ar thus respected, but the *maboya*.

In fact, as one might expect among a warli people, women were little esteemed, except mothers of future warriors. Columbus remark of the women he saw that they appeared to b mere servants and wives, and this seems to hav been so. In addition to the usual women's work Carib women were expected to carry all the load They spun the yarn from which hammocks wer made. As in other societies throughout the worl a good part of the wives' time was spent i attending to their husbands' personal needs. As w have seen, they combed and oiled his hair. I addition, they dressed him, and painted his body

Women and men lived separately, the women *carbet* being half the size of that in which the me lived. Women entered the men's *carbet* only t serve food to their husbands, standing in wait unt he had finished eating. Only then did they retur to the women's house for their own meal. Up t the age of four or five all children lived with thei mother, but at that age boys were taken away t live among the men. Girls remained with thei mothers until they married.

A Carib woman who was unhappy with her lo could do nothing to change it. If a husband wishe to abandon his wife at any time he could do so fo no reason. If the wife committed adultery, h could club her to death. We can imagine that woman captured by Caribs would be treated n better.

The Caribs and the sea

Drawn up on the beach near the village were the Caribs' all-important canoes, which might be up o 6 metres long. Like the Arawaks, the Caribs made these out of tree trunks. The trunk was charred, then hollowed with stone axes and left to season, after which it was buried in moist sand. Bars were placed across the opening to force out the sides, and were left in place until the wood had thoroughly dried and hardened. Then triangular boards were wedged at the bow and stern so that water could not enter the boat, and the sides were raised by fastening sticks bound with fibres and coated with gum to the upper edges. If this type of canoe overturned it did not sink, but instead could be righted by the paddlers and then vigorously rocked to splash out the water. The rest of the water was bailed out with calabashes. Some of these canoes had cabins in the centre in which the women lived when the family was travelling from one island to another.

Piragas were larger than the ordinary canoes. These were not dug-outs, but built with planks. Some were 12 metres long, and could carry 50 men. They had a raised and pointed bow and a *naboya* was painted on the stern to frighten away the enemy. Sometimes for additional decoration, a barbecued human arm was also fastened to the stern.

The Caribs had great respect for the ocean over which they so frequently travelled, and they took great care not to offend the spirits of the water for fear they would be harmed. They would eat no crab nor lizard while they were at sea, nor drink any water, for fear the spirits would be displeased and prevent them from reaching land. If they were carrying fresh water in the canoe, they took care not to spill any into the sea, as it might cause a storm. On the other hand, if they had to sail over a place where Caribs had drowned, they were careful to throw food into the water, so that the drowned men would not reach up to the boat and capsize it. When they were approaching land, they made sure not to call its name, nor to point to it, in case any evil spirit was watching and tried to prevent their getting ashore.

Because the Caribs depended upon their boats for their raiding and their food, the owner of a large canoe, or a *piraga*, was an important man. In time of war one of these *piraga* owners was chosen as 'admiral of the fleet' to command all the boats taking part in the raid. The *ouboutou*, or Great

Carib boat-building. Here the Carib men are charring the hollowed trunk of a tree.

Captain, however, who was the commander in chief of all the warriors, was elected for life. He was chosen because of his prowess in battle and his great strength, and was treated with great respect. The *ouboutou* was always accompanied by attendants, and everyone remained silent while he spoke. If any seemed lacking in respect, the attendants had the right to strike him. The *ouboutou* decided when the men would be called to the *carbet* to plan a raid. He decided also who should be attacked, and how the raid should be conducted, and when it would take place. He chose the commanders of the canoes and *piragas*. When the raid was over, and the men returned victorious, the *ouboutou* presided over the victory celebrations, during which everyone who had killed an Arawak chief was allowed to take his name as a mark of honour. It was during this celebration that the Arawak women who had been captured were given as wives to the bravest warriors. *Caracolis* were distributed to the young men who had distinguished themselves in battle, and these warriors were highly prized as husbands.

Sometimes Caribs ceremoniously killed and ate captive men. However, some of the captives were also kept as slaves. The women were given as concubines to warriors and the men kept as labourers. It is possible that some of these captive men married into their master's family since in some Carib languages the word *peiro*, which means slave, also means son-in-law. Children of slaves were born free.

Government in Carib society

Carib government was very simple. The *ouboutou* was the most important man among the Caribs, but they also had lesser governors for their villages, who ruled in times of peace. These men were called *tiubutuli hauthe*, and were the heads of families, for each family lived in its own village. Like the Arawak *cacique*, the *tiubutuli hauthe* supervised the fishing and cultivating, but he had very little authority beyond this. The Caribs disliked taking orders, and in fact they had very few laws. If anyone did injury to a Carib, the injured man was expected to take his own revenge without any interference from the rest of the tribe. He could even kill the person who had injured him. In fact, anyone who did not avenge himself when he was wronged was despised by his tribesmen as a weakling.

Another of the *tiubutuli hauthe's* important functions was to lead the village in ceremonies and entertainments of which the Carib were extremely fond. Wrestling, canoe racing, and especially singing, dancing and story-telling were favourite pastimes, and in all these he played a leading part. Certain occasions, such as a victory in war, a son's birth, or the launching of a new canoe, called for special feasts and drinking bouts, followed by games and dance and song.

The Carib were a people of great daring and courage, but these qualities could not save them. Their bows and poisoned arrows and their twelve metre long *pirogas* were to prove no match for the guns and armour of the Spaniards.

Things to do and think about

1 Find out all you can about any present-day Caribs in your country. If there is a museum visit it and see what you can learn about Carib life in the past.

2 Pretend you were an Arawak girl captured by the Caribs and describe your life. Or pretend you were a Carib boy and describe your initiation either as a warrior or as a priest.

3 Caribs sometimes caught fish by bruising a certain wood and poisoning the water. In how many different ways do fishermen in your country catch fish?

4 Compare the government and way of life of the Caribs with that of the Aztec and Maya. How do you account for the differences?

5 In what ways were the Caribs like the Arawaks? In what ways were they different?

6 Compare the Carib way of making a canoe with the way your fishermen make them. Are any canoes in your country big enough to hold 50 people?

7 Are there any Carib qualities which you admire? Which ones? Why? Why did they have to capture Arawak women?

8 Make a taumalin sauce and eat it with yam and sweet potato as the Caribs did.

9 What do you think probably happened when the Caribs saw Spanish ships approaching their shores?

10 From what you have learnt of the Caribs why might they consider that such occasions as a son's birth or the launching of a new canoe called for special festivities?

PART TWO

The Newcomers

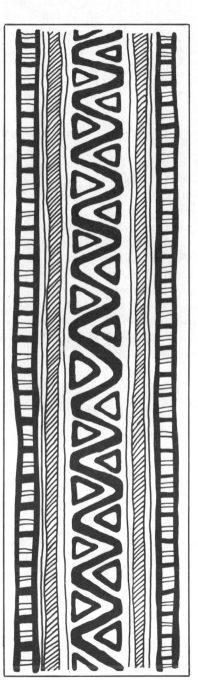

CHAPTER ELEVEN

The Africans

African Kingdoms

After the Spaniards had conquered the Indians of the New World in the sixteenth century, they enslaved them and forced them to mine for gold and silver to be sent to Spain. Under this harsh treatment the Indians died in great numbers, and the Spaniards, as well as other Europeans who followed them to the New World, sought labour in other places. They turned to Africa which they thought was peopled by savages. But Africa was far from being a savage place.

The great Arab traveller, Ibn Battuta, has left a description of the capital of the Negro Empire of *Mali*, or Melle, which he visited in the fourteenth century. He comments on the lavish use of gold worn as ornament and decorating the swords of the king's armour bearers, as well as the gold and silver guitars carried by the musicians who preceded him when he walked in state, and on the respect in which his subjects held him. Mali was established in about the eleventh century and continued until the fifteenth century when it collapsed after a succession of incompetent rulers. In the fifteenth and sixteenth centuries the *Songhai* Empire flourished, whose territory extended almost sixteen hundred miles eastward from the Atlantic coast. The *Ashanti* and the *Yoruba* kingdoms were flourishing when the first Portuguese explorers entered West Africa in the fifteenth century. And earlier than all these, had been the ancient kingdom of *Ghana*, founded about the eighth century, which continued strong and wealthy until it was conquered by the Almoravids from North Africa in the middle of the thirteenth century.

These large African states, however, developed only after many centuries of African history. For information on the thousands of years preceding their establishment, we must depend upon archaeology (as for the early history of all people and only now are African and other scholar beginning to discover much about Africa's distant past. Some archaeological evidence is already available, however. The rock paintings of the Sahara (you will remember seeing some of these in Chapter 1) tell us that at one time the parched desert was a fertile region supporting a hunting and farming population. Far to the south-east, a

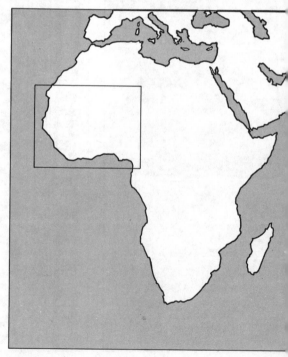

Africa.

Great Zimbabwe, are the ruins of a great temple whose 'dry-stone' walls (made of stones without the use of mortar) are 9 metres high (see page 65). Only a strong and stable government could have made such an enterprise possible, and historians now believe that the wealth of Great Zimbabwe was based on a mixture of gold and copper mining, cattle rearing and trade with the prosperous east coast of Africa. In West Africa, systems of agriculture were developed along the Upper Niger about six thousand years ago, and in West Africa, too, from about 200 B.C. the techniques of mining and smelting iron were known.

But because the Africans left no written records of their early history our knowledge is limited. Fortunately, we can piece some of this history together because tribes still exist who have passed down their own history from father to son by word of mouth over the centuries. We know, therefore, that Africa's early history was one of conquest and migration, with tribes constantly on the move, either seizing new lands, or fleeing invaders. Out of these movements of peoples developed the different types of African cultures – those of the forest hunters, the forest cultivators, and the settlers on the savannahs. As we would expect, the lives of these groups were greatly affected by their geographic conditions.

People of the forest

In the forest regions where trees can grow to heights of 60 metres with a circumference the size of a house, people turned to hunting. As a result, these people, as we have seen with the North American Indians, never developed settled communities, nor did they live in large tribal groups. Instead, a family or perhaps a few families would co-operate in the hunt, sharing the work, the dangers, the successes – and perhaps the hunger. In this small group it was not necessary to have a formal government, and decisions were reached after a general discussion in which the elders took an important part. Crime was almost unknown, but laziness was a serious offence, for if one failed to do one's share, all might starve. Punishment was also rare, but if it were needed, the most frequent method was to ridicule the offender until

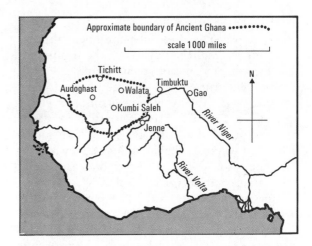

Ancient Ghana.

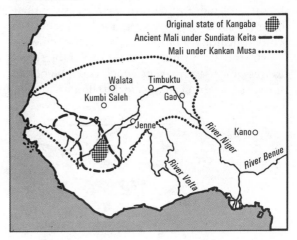

The expansion of the Empire of Mali.

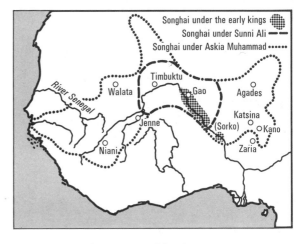

The expansion of the Empire of Songhai.

he changed his ways. If anyone did commit a crime, however, a dreadful punishment threatened him. He might be exiled from the group, and this, for a hunter, meant certain death.

Those who settled on the margins of the forest, however, were able to practise a simple type of agriculture. They felled trees with stone axes and fire, and practised a 'slash and burn' cultivation. The result was that, like the Iroquois, they had to leave their villages and set up new ones every few years as the fertility of the soil was exhausted. Villages were usually established when a leader first cleared the land and was acknowledged as the headman. Several families, all members of one clan, formed a village, and a characteristic of this society was that all inhabitants of the village were distantly related. Agriculture was the basis of their life, with the men clearing the land and the women planting and tending the crops, chief of which were (as with the Indians of South America) cassava, a starchy root which could be boiled or roasted, or dried and made into flour, plantain,

beans and peanuts. Sometimes, if the men were lucky, meat or fish was added to the diet. It was a hard life, for the forest, and the animals who lived in the forest, were a constant menace. Moreover, these forest-margin farmers lived in isolation, the forest itself forming a barrier to communication with other communities. These communities, therefore, remained small, devoting most of their skills and energies to the struggle for life.

People of the grasslands

For the settlers of the grasslands, however, the situation was very different. Here there were vast spaces to be farmed; the great rivers formed arteries of trade and transportation. There were no great natural obstacles separating one community from another. A determined leader, an ambitious and skilful warrior, could easily attack and conquer his weaker neighbours, and so establish control over a larger and larger region. Here,

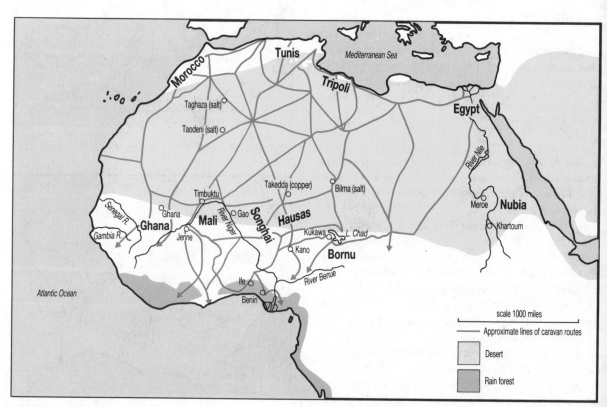

The Sahara Desert trade routes.

herefore, was where the great African kingdoms developed. Assured of a supply of food from their own fertile soil, having access to gold and to iron, these kingdoms grew rich on the thriving trade along the busy *trans-Sahara routes*, along which caravans carried goods between West and Northern Africa. Grain and cotton came from Egypt, silks from China, salt from the Sahara salt mines, thoroughbred horses and handwritten books from North Africa. From the cities of *Timbuktu, Jenne, Kano* and *Gao* went finely tooled leather and embroidered cotton cloth and, from the interior, kola nuts, ivory, ostrich plumes, gold and slaves, which were brought in great fleets of canoes down the Niger river. Although barter was widely practised, money was also used. This took the form of cowrie shells imported from East Africa, copper and iron bars of various standard sizes, and standard measures of gold dust.

The control of this trade was directly in the hands of the ruler who levied taxes on all imports

The ruins of Great Zimbabwe. These ruins date back to the fourteenth century. The walls are some of the best examples of the 'dry-stone' technique of construction in the world. Compare this picture to the one on page 25.

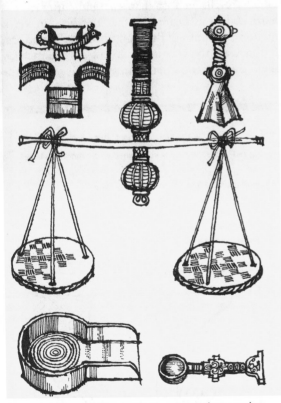

Instruments for weighing gold. The picture shows scales, weights and a shovel for the gold dust that are typical of the Ashanti society of modern day Ghana.

Ashanti gold weights. These weights were used by traders for measuring quantities of gold dust.

65

This splendid brass head represents an early Oni (ruler) of Ife. It was made in the 13th or 14th century.

and exports, and became extremely rich as a result. Much of the wealth was spent in the upkeep of a magnificent royal court, but much also was used for the expenses of running the government, and much was spent in employing artists who were maintained by the king and provided with the finest of materials with which they produced the magnificent work so admired today. They designed and hammered out the huge plaques, sometimes of solid gold, which adorned the walls of the royal dwellings; they carved the fantastic and awesome masks worn by the priests. Above all, using the 'lost wax' process they cast the magnificent bronze heads for which *Ife* and *Benin* were renowned.

In the lost wax process, wax is poured over a clay model roughly shaped like a human head. The features are then moulded on the wax, and small columns are attached to the top of the head and joined to a cup-shaped piece of wax above. The entire head is then covered with wet clay which is allowed to harden, and, after it has hardened, it is heated so that the wax inside is melted and runs out through a hole at the bottom. In this way, the wax inside is 'lost'. Inside the clay shell there is now an empty space where the

How bronze heads were cast by the 'lost wax' process.

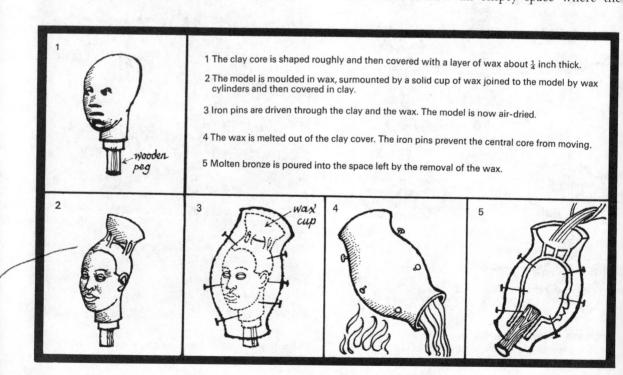

1 The clay core is shaped roughly and then covered with a layer of wax about ¼ inch thick.

2 The model is moulded in wax, surmounted by a solid cup of wax joined to the model by wax cylinders and then covered in clay.

3 Iron pins are driven through the clay and the wax. The model is now air-dried.

4 The wax is melted out of the clay cover. The iron pins prevent the central core from moving.

5 Molten bronze is poured into the space left by the removal of the wax.

cupshaped wax had been, and two channels where the wax tubes have melted. When molten bronze is poured into the space left by the wax it runs down these channels and settles around the features moulded on the side of the clay covering. When it has solidified, the outside clay is broken and the cast head is left.

Government in Africa

The African kingdoms of Ghana, Mali and Songhai existed at about the same time that Europe was going through that period we call the Middle Ages, and in some ways the two places had similar institutions. In Africa, for example, there existed a system which was similar to feudalism in Europe, in which rulers attempted to maintain stability within their territories through a system of mutual rights and duties. In Africa, as in Europe, this took the form of land given to certain chiefs or nobles to govern, in exchange for military service. In addition the chief was expected to pay tribute to the royal treasury, in the form of food, tools, leatherwork, or any other product of his province. On the other hand he was given almost complete control over his province, including the right to the labour of the farmers who could not leave the land without his permission. The position of these African farmers was similar to that of the European serf. There is also a similarity here, to many of the institutions we have read of among the Maya, Aztec and Inca.

Although all his chiefs owed him loyalty, however, and although he controlled the army, the power of the African ruler was limited by the fact that he was bound by the customs of his people. He could not act in such a way as to defy the traditions of the tribe, for this would incur the anger of the ancestors. We shall learn later of the great importance that ancestors played in the life of the African people. It was the duty of the elders and priests or witchdoctors to see that the ruler honoured tribal customs. In addition to being his advisers, the elders formed what we might call the Civil Service. They supervised collection of taxes, were responsible for seeing that all officials were paid, and supervised assistance to the poor. They were also, of course, the military leaders.

Religion in Africa

As important as the chiefs and elders, were the priests. They were not only advisers to the king, interpreters of the law, and the doctors; they were the guardians of the religious life of the people, without which it was felt the tribe could not survive. Among all African peoples religion played a vital part, and, although there were differences from one part of Africa to another, African religions had many similarities.

Like most of the peoples we have studied in this book, most Africans were polytheistic – believing in many gods. Each craft and trade was felt to have its own god, and, as they depended upon agriculture for their life they worshipped also gods of the earth, sky and sun, like *Shango*, the god of thunder whom the *Yoruba* people felt was also the special god of kings, and *Gu*, the Dahomey god of iron and war.

In addition to various gods, the Africans had a great reverence for their ancestors. This showed itself in ancestor worship and it was in these ceremonies that the bronze heads mentioned earlier were often used. Even powerful rulers were expected to follow the guidance of the ancestors, for it was felt that although dead, the ancestors still

Gu, the Dahomey god of iron and war.

67

Priests sometimes wore frightening masks such as this one.

was more specialised, had specialised duties. Artisans, for example, had to give a proportion of their work to the king's overseers as taxes; merchants paid a tax on all their imports and exports – the amount determined by the load carried by each beast of burden. Fishermen provided dried fish and farmers a certain amount of their produce for the king's storehouses. Some of this was used for the royal household, and some was put aside for the poor. Other people might have to provide servants for the ruler's household, or bodyguards for the king. Those dwelling near rivers might be called upon to provide canoes and paddlers for royal transport. The king of Songhai, when he conquered a tribe, demanded tribute of a hundred spears annually from each family of metal workers. In exchange, the inhabitants were guaranteed protection against outside attack. Moreover, they had some say in the government, for all free men had the right to take part in choosing the minor chiefs; they might even hope one day to become chiefs themselves.

had the well-being of the tribe at heart, and that their good-will could help the tribe – or their enmity could harm it.

For this reason, children's education was centred around learning the tribal customs and traditions so that they would live in a way which was pleasing to their ancestors. This training was in the hands of the priests. The children's education started very early and continued until they were about thirteen. At that time they went through a rigorous and secret initiation ceremony which tested their fitness to take part in all the activities of the community, and to accept the responsibilities of adulthood. Those who passed through this successfully were allowed to take part in the religious life of the people and, eventually, they too became elders whose voice was heeded with respect.

For slaves, however, the position was quite different. They were forced to remain in one place, and were limited to one definite occupation which was decided by the chief, or the king. Usually they formed the professional army. This was done so that the king could be certain his soldiers would remain in service and get regular training. People became slaves as a result of lawbreaking, or by capture in war, and sometimes these slaves were sold to Arab traders and taken along the trans-Sahara routes for sale in North or East Africa. As with the Aztec slaves we read about in Chapter 7, however, the slaves in Africa were sometimes able to earn enough to pay off their purchase price and buy themselves out of bondage. They could also marry into their owners' families, and some, who engaged in trade, became quite rich. It was even possible for a freed slave to become a chief.

Citizenship in Africa

The type of responsibility which was expected of an adult depended upon the type of community to which he belonged. As we might expect, those who lived in the large kingdoms, where society

Music in Africa

In all African communities, music held a very special place, for it was felt to have its own magic, which helped to bind all members of the community together. We read earlier of the gold and lver guitars used by musicians at the court of Mali. These were not typical of African instruments, however. In West Africa, the most characteristic instrument was (and is) the drum, of which here are many different kinds, used on different occasions. The best known of these are the great *Talking Drums*, which are used in pairs, and which imitate the sound of African speech, one drum producing a high note, and the other a low one. Using relays of drummers, messages could be quickly sent a hundred miles or more in this way.

Rhythm was the basis of all African music, but the drum was not the only instrument used to produce this rhythm. In fact, in some parts of Africa drums played a very minor role, and other instruments were widely used, made from materials readily available. Bamboo strips made xylophones; horn, wood, and tusks were fashioned into trumpets; calabashes and other gourds were turned into rattles. In Nigeria a special rattle called an *agbe* was made from a calabash from which all seeds had been removed, and around which was placed netting covered with cowrie shells. No one might use the *agbe* except the owner. A characteristic African instrument, made nowhere else, was the *sansa*, or thumb piano. This was made by hollowing out a piece of wood, and attaching a number of bamboo or metal strips over the hollow, and bending them over a bridge. The instrument was played by plucking the strips with the thumb. Sometimes the *sansa* was placed in a gourd which acted as a resonator.

Although these instruments were sometimes used alone, usually they were accompanied by singing and dancing. The healing services of the priests (for it must not be forgotten that many of them were doctors as well) took place to the rhythm of hand-clapping and chanting; marriage ceremonies were marked by festivities in which hundreds of participants danced and sang for hours on end; ritual dancing and songs marked the initiation ceremonies. Each craft and trade and occupation had its own songs, and recreation largely took the form of story-telling accompanied by singing and mime. Often the audience itself made up the choruses as the tale unfolded. The type of singing called leader and response, in which one person starts a song and the group sings a reply is typically African. A development of this

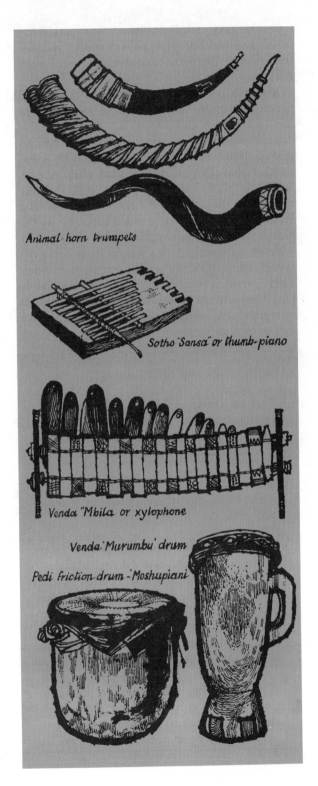

Animal-horn trumpets

Sotho 'Sansa' or thumb-piano

Venda 'Mbila' or xylophone

Venda 'Murumbu' drum

Pedi friction-drum-'Moshupiani'

Some African musical instruments.

type of singing, called antiphonal, was characteristic of medieval European church music, and it is thought that this might have been influenced from Africa.

Music is part of the cultural heritage of all peoples and in this way the African was similar to the Inca, Aztec and Maya, whose priests also danced and sang in their worship. The African priests, however, did not conduct their ceremonies from the platforms of lofty temples, but, attired in their awesome masks, invoked the blessings of the gods and the ancestors by dancing in the midst of reverent worshippers – as the North American Indian priests also did.

As we have seen, Africa was far from being the savage place the slave traders expected to find. There were a number of strong and stable kingdoms with a solid economic foundation based on agriculture, mining, metal work, and, above all, on trade with North Africa, Asia and Europe. Many Africans were very skilled artists, and the bronze figures from Nigeria are undoubtedly some of the finest statues in the world. African architecture made full use of local resources; imposing mosques were built in the prosperous trading towns of Jenne and Timbuktu, and further south, the 'dry-stone' walls of Great Zimbabwe are architectural masterpieces.

Like all people, however, the Africans had much to learn from others about new technologies and new ideas. Unfortunately, the traders who appeared from the west in the fifteenth century did not come to exchange goods and knowledge with the Africans. What they brought was greed and waiting ships, and the long nightmare of the middle passage to slavery on the plantations of the West Indies and North America.

Things to do and think about

1 Find on a map of Africa all the places mentioned in the chapter. What are the principal geographical features of these places?

2 What parts of Africa did most West Indians come from? What tribes did they belong to?

3 What modern African countries are found in places where Ancient Ghana, Mali, Songhai were established? In what African countries are the cities of Timbuktu, Gao, Kano, Benin and Jenne to be found?

4 Are any African customs still practised in your country? Are any African words used?

5 If there is a museum of African objects in your country visit it and note particularly the types of musical instruments. Try to make a *sansa* or an *agbe*. In what ways has African music made a contribution to the music of the West Indies and America?

6 What are the main products exported from West Africa today? What is the kola nut used for?

7 Pretend you were talking to a slave trader and try to convince him that Africans were not savages. Why do you think that slave traders would want to believe that Africans were uncivilised?

8 Compare the way the hunters in Africa controlled the group, with that of the Sioux. What are the reasons for which an African hunter might have been exiled?

9 Find out what you can about 'dry-stone' construction. What other people used this technique?

CHAPTER TWELVE

The East Indians

East Indians came to the Caribbean from India over a hundred years ago, and in some West Indian territories they now form about half the population. These East Indians are probably descended from the very early inhabitants of India who built up the *Indus valley* civilisation about four or five thousand years ago. This civilisation is so old that we know about it only through the work of archaeologists. They have discovered the remains of two great cities, *Mohenjo Daro*, and *Harappa*, and from the ruins of these cities they have learnt a great deal about how the early inhabitants of India lived.

The streets of these cities were broad and straight, and in the centre there was a large pool which was probably used for religious purposes. The dwelling houses were made of burnt bricks, and each house had a bathroom, and drainpipes

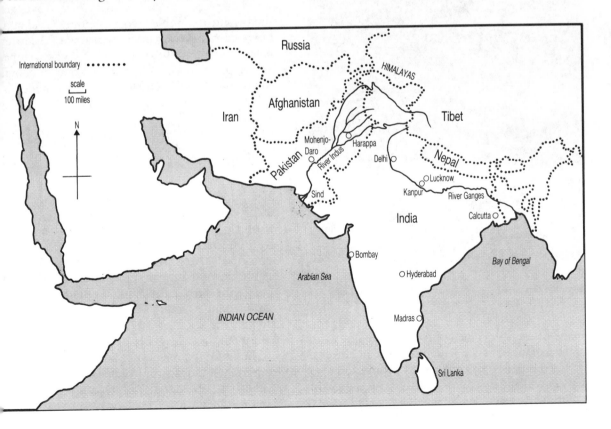

Prehistoric seals of the Indus Valley civilisations.

Siva, the Destroyer.

made of clay. Pots made of clay were also used, and decorations of copper, gold, silver and bronze were common. The people used bronze tools, so we know that they were well past the stone age. In addition, archaeologists have discovered many seals with writing on them, although they have not yet been able to decipher the writing. Perhaps these seals were used by merchants in signing their accounts.

Mohenjo Daro and Harappa seem to have been quite large cities, and since we know that people begin to live in cities only when they are sure of an adequate food supply, we know that agriculture must have been quite advanced in ancient India.

We cannot know very much about these early inhabitants until we can read their writing. However, we know that by 1300 B.C. they were attacked by a tribe called the Aryans, who swept down through India from *Afghanistan*. At first these Aryans were a 'barbarian' people who lived in huts of mud and wood with earthen floors covered with grass. They were farmers and kept animals of which the most important was the cow. A man's wealth was judged by the number of cows he owned. The richer people also kept horses which they used for pulling their chariots.

These Aryans were a warlike people who frequently fought among themselves. Their weapons were bows and arrows, spears, axes and slings, and the nobles wore armour. Gradually, however, the Aryans intermarried with the original inhabitants of the Indus Valley, and developed a more peaceful life. Over the years they, too, built towns and cities. Their cities were surrounded by moats and walls, like medieval European castles, and were ruled by kings.

Two great religions

The Aryans at first worshipped gods of nature such as fire, thunder, the sun, and the dawn. They wrote their beliefs in poems called the *Vedas*. Over the centuries, however, the inhabitants of India developed a new religion known as *Hinduism*. This is the oldest organised religion in the world, and it differs from all the other religions in that it has no single founder, such as Abraham, or Buddha, or Jesus, or Muhammad, and no single holy book like the Bible or the Koran.

Hinduism is a religion of many gods, the most important of which are *Brahma*, the Life-giver; *Vishnu*, the Preserver; and *Siva*, the Destroyer. Hindus believe that the only way to be happy is to have a pure and perfect soul. They believe that in order to achieve this, people are reborn many times after death, and that a bad person is reborn into a lower caste, or even as an animal. For this reason, Hindus respect all animals and will not eat meat. After many rebirths, the Hindus believe the soul becomes pure and perfect and is united with the god, Brahma. When this happens there is no need for any more rebirths.

The caste system became important in the Hindu religion because there were many ceremonies to be performed. The priests, or *brahmins*, who performed these ceremonies were members of the highest caste. Below them were the warriors, then the merchants, then the workmen. *Sudras*, or slaves were at the bottom, and below even these were those who were so despised that they were called *Untouchables*. No one, not even a slave, would associate with the Untouchables, or even touch what they had handled.

As we learn more about India we shall see that religion has always played an important part in her history. We have learnt that the oldest organised religion in the world started in India. *Buddhism*, which is the second largest religion in the world today, also began in India. Its founder was a prince's son called *Suddhartha Gautama*.

Gautama was born into the Hindu faith, but as a young man he became very distressed at the suffering and injustice he saw about him, especially among members of the lower castes of Hindus. He asked the Hindu priests to explain to him why people should suffer, and how unhappiness could be prevented, but they were unable to do so. He then determined to live the life of a holy man, and try to find the answers for himself. He left his wife and baby son and comfortable home, and travelled about India, living in poverty, and always seeking to find the answer to his questions. Over the years he gathered many disciples around him, and when he felt he had found the answers he taught it to them. They called him the *Buddha*, or *Enlightened One*, and after his death they continued his teachings.

Buddha's teachings are called the 'Four Noble Truths'. He taught that all men are equal, and that all men can lead a holy life – there need not be special priests. People are unhappy, said the Buddha, because they want too many things. If they would cease to desire wealth and comfort

they would not be unhappy. Furthermore, people must respect all life. They must not kill any living thing, not even the smallest insect. They must not lie, or steal, or speak evil of others. These are the simple rules on which Buddhism is founded.

Buddha did not mean to form a new religion, and Buddhists believed in the same gods as the Hindus. However, many people preferred his teaching to the old Hindu religion with its emphasis on caste, and eventually Buddhism became the chief religion of Asia. Many men and women became Buddhist monks and nuns, and lived in monasteries where they devoted their whole lives to religion. Often these monks and nuns became missionaries who carried Buddhist teachings to other lands. They shaved their heads, as Buddha had done, and wore yellow robes, and carried only a rough wooden bowl with which they begged for food.

Buddha.

The first great kings

We see that the religions of Hinduism and Buddhism were important in Indian history. Later we shall see that Islam also played a part. Meantime, however, let us follow the story of India from its early days and see what happened in that vast country over the thousands of years until East Indians came to the Caribbean.

Because India has such a long history we find that it was ruled differently at different times. Sometimes most of the country was united under one ruler, at other times the ruler was weak, and Indians warred among themselves for hundreds of years. Sometimes the rulers were Indians; at other times they were foreign invaders who had conquered India.

The first great Indian king was called *Chandragupta*. He ruled for over seventy years, from 396–321 B.C. This was about two hundred years after Buddha was born. Chandragupta built himself a great capital city which was surrounded by a wooden wall with sixty-four gates, and seven hundred and fifty towers to defend it against attack. In the centre of this city stood the royal palace, and surrounding the palace were inns, markets, and other dwelling houses, some of them three storeys high. Chandragupta was a strong ruler who united most of India for the first time, and built good roads to connect the various cities within his empire. However, he was disliked by the people for he ruled by fear. He kept a large army, and many secret police whose duty it was to spy on the people and report anyone who criticised the king. In fact, so much did the people hate him that he sometimes changed his bedroom in the middle of the night to confuse anyone who might want to kill him.

Chandragupta was not killed, however, but died naturally, and the next great king after him was his grandson *Asoka*. Unlike his grandfather, Asoka was loved by the people, for he ruled for their benefit. Instead of relying on secret police to tell him what was happening, he appointed governors of the provinces who heard the people's complaints, and tried to remedy conditions. He had many hospitals built, and he released many of the people that Chandragupta had imprisoned so that they could live useful lives once more.

It was under Asoka that Buddhism spread throughout India. In his early years he had been a great warrior and conqueror, and shortly after he became king he conquered the kingdom of *Kalinga* in which his soldiers killed a hundred thousand people. However, he soon repented of this evil deed, and determined that he would fight no more. He became a Buddhist, and sent Buddhist missionaries throughout his empire, and even to distant places like Egypt, Ceylon, Syria and Greece. He did not force the people to accept Buddhist teaching, but in order to make sure that they could learn about it he had great stone pillars built on which these teachings were carved. The writings on these pillars are the first Indian writings which we are able to read.

Unfortunately, when Asoka died there was no good strong ruler to succeed him, and India once more went through a long period of wars. Then a family called the *Gupta* started another dynasty.

Under the Gupta rulers (A.D. 350–500) India became the most civilised country of that time. In addition to beautiful painting and sculptures, they excelled in mathematics. It was the Indians who discovered the importance of zero, and who developed a simple way of writing numbers. This knowledge was brought to Europe by the Arabs during the Middle Ages.

They were made like this in India more than 1,000 years ago. Notice the zero.

The Arabs make them like this.

Caxton, the Englishman, first printed them like this.

Numbers one to ten in three different languages. This shows clearly how the system developed from the Indians.

During the reign of one of the Gupta emperors, a Chinese pilgrim named *Fa H'sien* travelled through northern India to visit holy places connected with Buddha's life, for Buddhism had now spread to China. Here is what *Fa H'sien* saw during his travels:

'The people are rich and happy. Only those who plough the king's land have to pay much on the profit they make. Those who want to go away, may go; those who want to stay, may stay. The king in his government gives no punishments by beating; criminals are merely fined according to the seriousness of their offences. Even for a second attempt at rebellion the punishment is only the loss of the right hand. Throughout the country no one kills any living thing, nor eats onions nor garlic, nor drinks wine. In this country they do not keep pigs or fowls; there are no dealings in cattle, no butcher shops, or distilleries in their market places. As a medium of exchange they use cowries.'

The coming of the invaders

Fa H'sien visited India when the Guptas were strong and there was peace. However, India was attacked in A.D. 500 by a vicious tribe from the north known as the Huns, who murdered and destroyed what the Guptas had built, and in about A.D. 1000, India was invaded by the Turks, who then ruled the country for several centuries.

We read earlier that the religion of Islam influenced Indian history. This was introduced by the Turkish invaders, many of whom ruled India very harshly. Under some of these Turk, or Mogul, rulers, the Indian Hindus were discriminated against and had to pay extra taxes, while people who were Muslims were exempt. Ibn Battuta, the North African who travelled over much of Asia in the fourteenth century, has left us a picture of what India was like under one of the Mogul rulers, Sultan Muhammed. Ibn Battuta said, 'Every day one man receives a fortune from the Sultan – but every day another man loses his head.'

However, Sultan Muhammed also did some good things for India. He had good roads built, along which his messengers could travel as, like those of the Inca, they carried reports or taxes from the various cities of the empire. Each messenger, as he ran, carried a stick on which were three bells. At intervals of a third of a mile along the roads rest houses were built, and as each runner approached the rest house he rang his bell and a fresh runner made ready to relieve him. So the message passed from hand to hand, and took only five days to go from the Indus to *Delhi* by king's messenger. A good team of runners could cover two hundred miles in one day on the royal roads. But these roads could not be used by the ordinary people, and for them to go from the Indus to Delhi might take several weeks.

All sorts of trade was carried on in India at this time, even a trade in wives. Ibn Battuta told how you could 'buy a cow for three silver dinars, and a pretty wife for a gold dinar.'

Some of the Mogul rulers, like the great *Akbar*, were among India's great kings. Akbar was only thirteen years old when he became king, and until he was twenty he was more interested in hunting and games than he was in ruling the country. When he began to take his rule seriously, however, the Indian people were grateful for his government. One of the first things he did was to abolish the tax on Hindus. Even more important, he checked up on his tax-collectors, to make sure that they were only collecting the proper amount of tax, and not robbing the people to make themselves rich.

Part of the money which Akbar collected in taxes was spent in increasing educational opportunities for the people. He wanted every boy in India to be able to read and write, and he was especially interested that they should read books on their country's history. Akbar did many other things for India. He established a postal service for all the people, using camels for transport. He encouraged trade. One interesting experiment he made was to try to establish a new religion which was a mixture of Hinduism and Islam. He called it the *Divine Faith*, and he hoped that the new religion would help to unite all the people of India. Unfortunately he did not succeed, and the Hindus and Muslims of India remain divided even today.

But although Akbar did not succeed in uniting Muslims and Hindus into one faith, there was a tribe, the *Sikhs*, in north India, who did succeed in doing so. They felt there was good in both religions, and set up their own religion which combined a little of both. Their religion preached belief in one God, and was opposed to idolatry and the caste system. Akbar's successors persecuted the Sikhs very severely until they formed themselves into a group with military discipline, for their own protection. This discipline is called the *Khalsa*, and exists even today. The Khalsa enforced very severe rules for all Sikhs. For example, every male Sikh had to take the name Singh, meaning lion, and had to wear five badges of his faith: the *khanga*, or comb; the *kachch*, or shorts; the *kara*, or iron bangle; the *kirpan*, two-edged sword; and long hair which he wore tucked under a turban.

The Khalsa was formed during the reign of *Shah Jahan*, Akbar's grandson, who was interested mainly in collecting money to build a magnificent court. In one of his palaces was the beautiful Peacock Throne which cost millions of pounds to build, and was studded with diamonds, rubies, pearls and emeralds. It took over seven years to make. It was *Shah Jahan*, too, who built the *Taj Mahal* as a tomb for his wife. Twenty thousand workmen spent fifteen years to build this tomb which cost millions. A visitor to India has described how the ordinary people were living while the emperor was spending millions on luxuries:

'There are in India many signs of poverty and hardship. Even the fertile districts are frequently untilled, owing to lack of labourers, many of whom die of the treatment they receive from their rulers. Often, if they cannot pay everything their greedy lords demand, their farms are taken from them, and sometimes, even, their children are sold as slaves.'

No wonder the people of India were dissatisfied, and sometimes disloyal to their ruler. Nor were the rulers or the people of India noticing what was happening in the world outside. They did not realise that European traders were hungri-

The Taj Mahal, built by Shah Jahan as a tomb for his wife.

eyeing India's wealth. They did not know that when the Portuguese set up a trading station at Goa in the sixteenth century, they would be followed by other foreigners, and that before long India would be once more invaded and ruled from a foreign land. This time the invaders were the English, and India remained a British colony from the eighteenth century until she once more became independent in 1947. It was while the English were ruling India in the nineteenth century that the first East Indians left their shores to come to the Caribbean.

A Sikh, standing in front of the Golden Temple of Amritsar, the holiest place in the Sikh religion.

Things to do and think about

1 Find out when Indians first came to your country. What did they come to do? What part of India did they come from? Are any of them named Singh? Are they Sikhs?

2 Are any Indian customs practised in your country? If you are not Indian, try and take part in an Indian celebration and explain what it is like. What is Indian music like? Describe the instruments.

3 Are there any Buddhists or Muslims in your country? What are their holidays? What is their worship like?

4 Find out all you can about Buddha, and write a story or act a play about his life.

5 Pretend you were a Hindu who heard Buddha teaching. Write a story telling what he taught and whether or not he convinced you to change your religion from Hinduism to Buddhism.

6 Describe life in India under Chandragupta or under Akbar.

7 Make a model of the Taj Mahal. If you were to put up a pillar with Christian teachings, what are some of the important things you would write on it?

8 Who was St Francis Xavier? Find out what connection he had with India.

9 Find out all you can about India and Pakistan today. Find them on the map. Which country were they both part of originally? Why are there two countries today?

CHAPTER THIRTEEN

The Chinese

Very old Chinese legends say that in the beginning of the world there were twelve Emperors of Heaven who were gods, and that each of these ruled for eighteen thousand years. After that time, the legends say, there were eleven Emperors of Earth who also ruled for eighteen thousand years each. Then there were nine Emperors of Mankind, but these ruled for only five thousand years each. These were followed by Kings, and one of these became the Yellow Emperor, or first Emperor of China, whose wife taught the Chinese to keep silkworms, and to make silk.

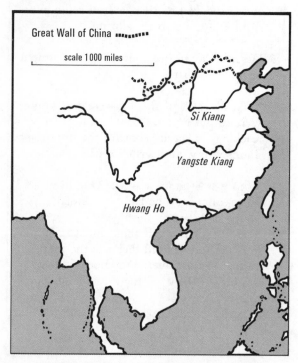

China: the great rivers.

Of course these are only legends. But we d know quite a lot about the true history of earl China, for archaeologists have dug up the ruins very old cities in the *Hwang Ho* River valley. these ruins they have found many artefacts an farming implements made of bronze, as well fine pots of fire-hardened clay. They have als found writing done by these ancient Chinese wh lived over three thousand years ago. This writin was done on tortoise-shell or bone, or on bambo strips, for the Chinese did not yet know how t make paper.

For thousands of years after this, the Chines were ruled by different families or dynasties. W shall read in this chapter about some of thes dynasties, and how they helped to make China th richest country in the world. The most importan of the Chinese dynasties were those of *Ch'in*, *Han Tang*, *Sung* and *Ming*. The Ch'in were the famil who gave their name to China when they invade it from the north-west in 221 B.C.

The Ch'in Dynasty

Before the Ch'in conquest the country had bee disturbed by wars among the many nobles. *Shi Huang Ti*, the Ch'in ruler, forced these nobles t give up all their weapons, which he melted dow to make statues for his palace. More important, h forced all the people to write letters in the sam way so that the Chinese language could be read b anyone in his Empire. Until this was done, it wa possible for people in the same country to feel the were speaking two different languages, for th same word was pronounced differently in differ ent districts. For example, the written character O means sun, but it can be pronounced either *Jih* or *Yat*. However, once the letters looked the same, all people throughout the Empire could read, and this helped to unite the country.

The Emperor Shih Huang Ti's other contribution to China was the completion of the *Great Wall* along China's northern border. It climbed over mountains and twisted through valleys for two thousand four hundred kilometres. In some places it rose 9 metres in height, and at the top it was 4.5 metres wide so that chariots could drive along it. In the thousands of towers built along the wall, sentries were posted to watch and warn against attack. At the first sign of hostile horsemen these sentries sent smoke signals by day, or lit great bonfires at night. It took eleven years to build this gigantic wall, and over three hundred thousand Chinese laboured on it. Many died of overwork, or exposure from the summer heat or winter cold, and they hated the Emperor who forced them to leave their homes and families to work and die in this bitter place. So, after his death, they rose in revolt.

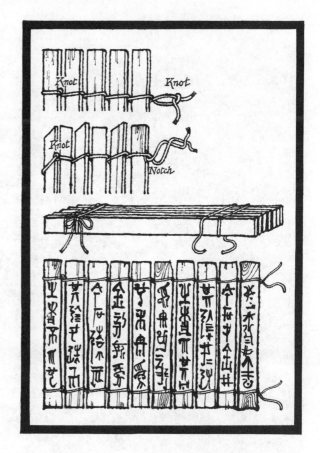

How an ancient Chinese book was put together.

These examples show how the Chinese altered their form of writing.

Now see how new words were made by putting other pictograms together.

The earliest forms of Chinese writing were based on pictograms – simple picture signs.

The Great Wall of China, completed after eleven years in the reign of Emperor Shih Huang Ti of the Ch'in dynasty.

The Han Dynasty

One of the leaders of this revolt was named *Han*, and he started a dynasty which brought peace to China for over four hundred years. One of the most important discoveries made under Han rule was the possibility of improving the fertility of the soil by crop rotation. Improved yields meant prosperity for the farmers. Other discoveries, too, made the farmer's life easier. They learnt, for example, to use a breastplate harness for their draught animals so that they could more easily pull the plough without tiring, and so more land could be brought under cultivation. And these discoveries were not confined to agriculture. During the Han dynasty the Chinese learnt how to make paper from rags. Astronomers worked out an accurate calendar which the Chinese continued

to use for two thousand years. Scientists invented the first seismograph – an instrument by which earthquakes could be measured. An important discovery, which was made by mistake, was that of gunpowder. People tried to turn lead into gold but instead of getting the precious metal they got an explosion. For many years they used this gunpowder only for fireworks.

The Tang Dynasty

When the last Han Emperor died, China once more went through a long period of warfare. For over three centuries the country was weakened by civil war, and then for nearly a century more it was ruled by strong but despotic rulers. Finally, in the seventh century A.D., another family began to rule

China and continued to govern for nearly three hundred years. This was the *Tang* dynasty.

The Tang emperors built a huge city for their capital which was called *Ch'ang An*. It had a population of two million people and was the largest city in the world. Surrounding the city was a high square wall with brick towers at the corners, and gates through which passed merchants, and government officials, soldiers, tradesmen, farmers, messengers – people from all over China and the world outside. They brought food for the inhabitants, and taxes they had collected for the emperor. They brought rolls of silk cloth for the wealthy merchants and the merchants' wives to wear. They brought ivory from Africa, rhinoceros horn from India, as well as gold, pepper and furs.

Under the Tang rulers the custom started of choosing government officials from among young men who had passed a very difficult examination in Chinese history, law, mathematics, and above all in the teachings of *Confucius*. This examination was held every three years, and any boy, no matter how poor his family, could sit for it, and, if he succeeded, he could rise to a very high position. It was easier than before to study under the Tangs, for in their reign the art of printing was discovered. Up to then, all books had been written by hand using brushes made of rabbit hair, or even mouse whiskers. Now, however, the characters, or letters, were carved on a block of wood, and then transferred to paper by inking the block. The letters were set in a frame, and a whole page could be printed at once. The earliest printed book we know of is called the *Diamond Sutra*, and was printed during the Tang dynasty.

Confucius, whose teachings were required for the examination, had lived many centuries before the Tang, but his teachings were so wise that they were followed by many thoughtful Chinese. He had lived during a time of great troubles and warfare, and spent many years trying to discover a way in which people could live happier and more peaceful lives. Finally, he came to the conclusion that a country could only be happy if all the people from the ruler down lived an honourable and upright life. He taught that good life began with the family. If the father of a family was a loving and upright man, his family would be happy. If there were upright and happy families in a country the country would be peaceful and prosperous. He taught that a ruler was like the father of his people, and that if he gave his people love and protection they would respect and love him in return. One day, when a greedy ruler complained to Confucius that many of his people were robbers, Confucius replied, 'Because you are greedy. When the ruler is bad, the people are also bad. A ruler is like the wind; his people are like the grass.' Confucius' teachings were written in books called the *Lu Yu*, or *Analects*.

The Sung Dynasty

Unfortunately, the later Tang emperors forgot Confucius' wise teachings, and oppressed their people so that China grew weak. Once more, she was invaded by barbarians, and the people suf-

Confucius, from an old steel engraving.

fered long years of warfare. Then, another dynasty was established, known as the *Sung*. Under the Sung rulers China once more went through a period of greatness. Under this rule, which lasted from A.D. 960–1279, the Chinese became some of the world's greatest traders. They sailed their *junks* as far as East Africa, to which they sent tea and silk and porcelain in exchange for ivory. Much of this trade was in the hands of Arabs, who liked to deal with the Chinese for they had a great reputation for being honest in business and keeping their promises.

The junks in which goods were carried to and from China were large enough to hold more than six hundred men. In fact, the traveller Ibn Battuta described junks that carried six hundred sailors and four hundred soldiers and were four storeys high. He told how the sailors grew their vegetables for the long voyages in clay and wooden pots aboard the ship. These junks had sails and were steered with rudders at the stern. Their anchors were made of stone. Merchants who travelled on them paid for their purchases with copper coins called *cash*, or with paper money. The cash were round coins with a square hole in the centre through which a string was passed.

By the time of the Sung rulers most Chinese followed the Buddhist religion which they had learnt from the Indians as a result of travels by men like Fa H'sien. These Buddhist travellers also helped to increase trade, for they brought China information about India and other places and helped to establish trade routes. The Buddhist monasteries were used as banks where merchants could keep their valuables and their money.

During the Sung period a very wise adviser to the Emperor tried to bring about certain social and economic improvements. His name was *Wang Ah Shih*, and he felt the government should run the country's agriculture, trade and industry so that the poor people would benefit. He encouraged lending money direct to farmers so that they need not pay high interest to money-lenders. The farmers used the money to buy seed, and repaid it towards the end of the year when they had harvested and sold their crop. In addition, Wang Ah Shih had canals built so that farmers could irrigate their fields, and he fixed the prices of essential foods and other goods so that the merchants could not profiteer. Workers in the towns also benefited, for he set up a committee to decide on fair wages and to determine the amount of old people's pensions.

The people, however, were expected to give something in return for these benefits. Sometimes they had to provide labour on public works. But Wang Ah Shih also allowed them to pay a small tax instead of labour if they wished, so that they need not leave their farms or shops. He also insisted that every family send one man to serve in the army, and divided the country into groups of ten families with a leader responsible for the behaviour of each group.

Unfortunately, Wang Ah Shih made enemies among the landlords and other rich people, who persuaded the Emperor to dismiss him from his post. Once more the people became dissatisfied. Eventually, however, China was invaded by the

Chinese junks of the Sung Dynasty.

Mongols, the most famous of whom was *Kublai Khan*. He was ruling China when *Marco Polo*, the Venetian merchant, visited there in A.D. 1274. Here is Marco Polo's account of what he saw:

'Kublai Khan did not forget the poor; every day his servants gave away twenty thousand bowls of food. When harvests were bad, men bought rice and millet cheaply from the Khan's storehouses. So, even in bad years, farmers had food and seed-grain.

The streets of *Camabaluc* [Peking] are wide and straight, and they cross at right angles. There are wide roads all through China. Trees are planted at the sides so that a man cannot stray from the road at night. Important messages can be sent quickly.

In the south is the city of *Hangchow*. It measures a hundred miles round. Twelve thousand stone bridges cross its canals. The Chinese bathe every day and they always wash their hands before they eat – you laugh and say this is not true! They heat their water and cook their food on fires of black stones out of hillsides. The black stones are useless for building but they throw out a great heat.'

The Ming Dynasty

Kublai Khan died in A.D. 1294 but China continued to be ruled by the Mongols until 1350, when they were replaced by another Chinese dynasty called the *Mings*. At first the Mings were very progressive, and Chinese junks traded widely in South-East Asia and as far as East Africa. However, in 1430, for some strange reason, all this was changed. The Emperor forbade trade with foreigners except through the city of *Canton*, and China found herself increasingly cut off from the rest of the world.

Most Chinese did not notice much change in their lives, however. The very wealthy continued to live in their beautiful homes surrounded by courtyards and gardens, where they were waited upon by many servants, and ceremonially drank steaming tea from thin porcelain cups. Jugglers, acrobats, musicians and story-tellers entertained them. Special teachers, who lived with the family, prepared their sons for the government examination. Their wives and daughters swayed gently as they strolled through the gardens on their tightly

Chinese ladies of the mid Sung dynasty ironing newly woven silk.

bound feet, their long, brightly varnished finger-nails just showing beneath the sleeves of their flowing silk gowns.

The poor, too, especially those in the country, found life too hard to worry about the new law passed in Peking. Men and women laboured in the fields growing rice, millet and barley. Each family planted a few tea bushes, which they tended carefully, for there was competition among the farmers to see whose tea would be of the highest quality. Tea drinking was very popular among the wealthy Chinese, but the poor could not afford it, because a special tax was placed on tea. Often the farmers had to leave their fields to labour in the government mines or on other public works, for which they were often not paid. Taxes were heavy, and were often collected by dishonest men who kept a large part for themselves. As a result,

many Chinese farmers were so poor that they had to sell some of their children into slavery in order that the rest of the family might live. They prayed for strong and honest rulers who would bring peace and justice, for they agreed with Confucius that, 'A cruel ruler is more terrible than a tiger.'

By the middle of the fifteenth century, therefore, China was no longer a developing country. She had given many things to the world: the mariner's compass, the printing press, paper, gunpowder. But from the fifteenth century China seemed to stand still while Europe used these discoveries and inventions to make herself rich and powerful, and to send her seamen and soldiers throughout the world. In the nineteenth century Europeans entered China as conquerors, and in 1837 the first Chinese went from Asia to the West Indies as labourers.

Things to do and think about

1 Are there any Chinese in your country? Find out when they came there and why. Do they practise any special customs, or have they any special celebrations?

2 Find out all you can about Kublai Khan and Confucius.

3 Using a brush, try to write a sentence in printed letters. Can you see why it would take a Chinese child a long time to learn to write well?

4 Using strips of bamboo try to make a book like the one on page 79. Paint on it examples of all the kinds of writing you have learnt about – Maya, Aztec, Indian and Chinese. Get your teacher to show you examples, also, of Egyptian *hieroglyphic* and Mesopotamian *cuneiform* writing, so that you can include these in your book.

5 What do you think was the most important event or discovery which took place during the following dynasties: Ch'in, Han, Sung, Ming.

6 Which do you think was more important: the discovery of printing or gunpowder? Give your reasons.

7 Does your government do any of the things which were suggested by Wang Ah Shih? Do any people object to these things? Which of the South American Indian people had a form of government similar to that set up by Wang Ah Shih?

8 Chinese Civil Servants were appointed as a result of their success in the government examination. Do you think this was a good idea? How are Civil Servants appointed in your country?

9 Find out all you can about China today. Imagine you are a news reporter who has just come back. Write a report on China today.

CHAPTER FOURTEEN

The Europeans

To the men of the New World, Africa and Asia, Europeans came as explorers and conquerors. By the late fifteenth century they were the most technically advanced people in the world. Using knowledge which had come to them from others,

Europeans added to it by experiment and invention until they had improved upon the original ideas. Thus they improved the *mariner's compass* so that they were able to determine their position when they were far from land. They developed the art of using gunpowder in firearms, so that they could easily overcome superior numbers.

The development of European shipping.

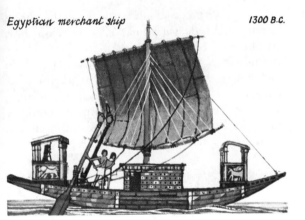

Egyptian merchant ship   1300 B.C.

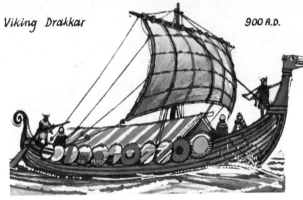

Viking Drakkar   900 A.D.

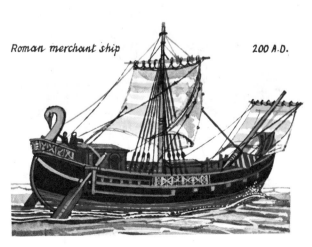

Roman merchant ship   200 A.D.

N. Mediterranean ship   1250 A.D.

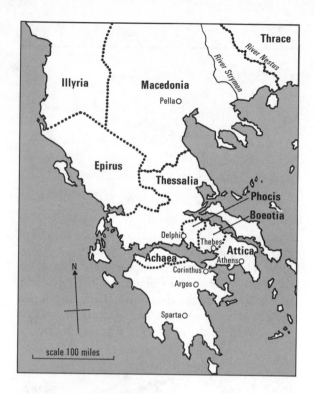

Macedonia and the main Greek States.

Ruins of the Parthenon, in Athens. Built nearly 2,500 years ago, this is considered to be one of the finest examples of classical architecture.

They developed the printing press so that accurate maps of distant places were more cheaply and readily available to their seamen. In addition, by the sixteenth century, Europeans had made some important technical discoveries of their own. Because they used the *pulley*, the *winch* and the *capstan*, they could manage the heavy rigging on their ships with smaller crews, which meant that less food and water had to be carried on long journeys.

Yet the Europeans had been the last of the Old World continents to develop a civilisation. While the Egyptians had been building pyramids in North Africa, and the great city of *Mohenjo Daro* was flourishing in India, the men of Europe were still 'barbarians'. Like all people, however, they slowly learnt the arts and skills of civilisation.

The ancient civilisations

In about 1400 B.C. a people we now call the *Greeks* began, in the *Balkan peninsula*, to develop these arts. Like the Maya, they lived in small city-states. Because there were only a few thousand people in each state, it was possible for them to practise what we may call 'direct democracy'. Each citizen could vote and debate on how his government should be run. But the Greeks felt that a good citizen should be interested in more than politics. A good citizen

hould be well educated in music, dancing and
port, as well as in reading, mathematics and
ublic speaking. The *Olympic Games*, which the
Greeks first started, produced many fine athletes;
while others excelled in drama, poetry, sculpture,
architecture and scientific enquiry. Over two
thousand years ago, a Greek calculated the size of
the earth and discovered that it was round.

In the fourth century B.C., however, the Greek
city-states began quarrelling among themselves
and the wars which followed destroyed them. But
what they had made, discovered and developed,
lived on.

Meanwhile, another people had established a
city-state – *Rome* – on the banks of the river *Tiber*.
By the first century A.D., Rome had become the
centre of the best-governed Empire in the ancient
world. The Romans made laws for themselves and
the people they conquered; and they built roads
and buildings which we still use and have with us
today.

The Middle Ages in Europe

After about three hundred years, however, the
Roman Empire began to decline, and it was
invaded by new warlike people from northern
Europe. For nearly two centuries these invaders

Ruins of the Colosseum in Rome, first built 2,000 years ago.

The Roman Empire, showing the Latin names for the
provinces of the Empire.

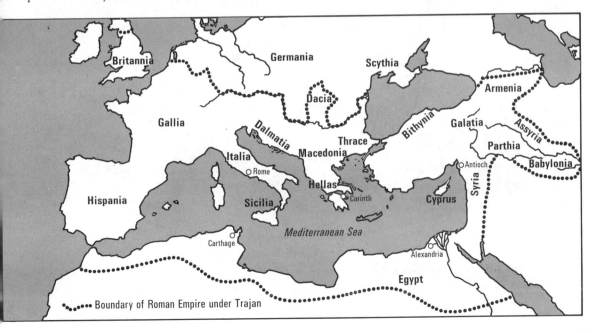

87

fought each other for the old Empire. Eventually, however, the northern tribes settled down under the control of strong chieftains or kings, although the conflicts between them continued for several centuries more. During this period of unrest, the *feudal system* developed. We have already seen a kind of feudal system among the Inca and some of the African kingdoms. In western Europe, the king or lord granted lands to lesser nobles who then became his *vassals*. Vassals had to fight in the king's wars and pay his ransom if he were captured in battle. The fighting men of the king and his vassals were armed horsemen, called *knights*.

Under this system, the majority of the people, who were farmers, became what we call *serfs* or unfree labourers. They had to provide food for the king, his lords and the knights; and their wives became the household servants of the 'upper' class. For this they received no payment. But in time of danger they could seek protection behind the thick stone walls of the lord's castle. The feudal system lasted for several hundred years in Europe, but it fell apart when it became clear that it was not suitable for countries wanting to expand their political and economic power.

A medieval castle. During the Middle Ages there were hundreds of such castles in Europe. Why do you think they were built in this way?

Religious wars – the Crusades

Many of the wars of this time (which we call the *Middle Ages*) were fought because of religion. Even before the fall of Rome, many people had been converted to *Christianity*. Now all the kings of Europe, from about A.D. 500, were Christian and they felt that the rest of the world should be Christian also. They set out from time to time on *Crusades*. These were wars fought against another people, the Arabs and Moors of North Africa, who had adopted a different religion. This was *Islam*, or the *Muslim* religion, whose founder was called *Muhammad*. The Muslims, as convinced as the Christians that theirs was the only true faith, had set out to conquer the world. They invaded India as we saw in Chapter 12, over-ran all North Africa, and conquered most of Spain by A.D. 760. They had also captured *Jerusalem*, which the Christians regarded as a Holy City, since *Jesus Christ* had been crucified there.

But the Crusades and the long conflict between Christian and Arab did not bring only bloodshed. The Arabs were a highly civilised people. They had a fine culture of their own. They had also been trading with India and China for centuries (when the European kings had been fighting among each other); and they had also learnt a great deal from the Greeks. Now, during the Crusades, Christian

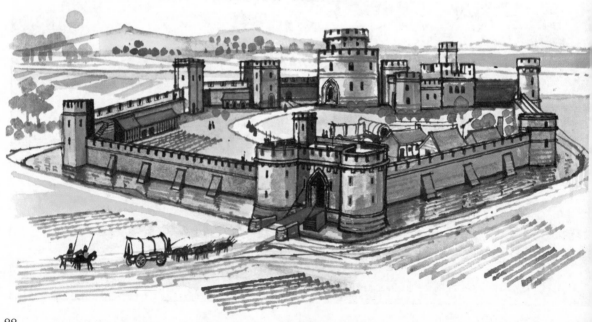

oldiers and merchants began to learn from the Muslims. What specially interested some European scholars was the Arabs' mathematics and scientific learning – especially the theory that the earth was not flat (as the Christian Church taught), but round (as the Greeks had discovered).

The conflict with Islam also meant that trade within Europe itself began to flourish. After the fall of Rome, there had not been much buying and selling in Europe. Times were too unsettled. But now merchants had to supply the Crusaders with food, arms and clothing. Markets, then market-towns, began to spring up. When the European merchants saw what lovely things the Arab merchants could obtain from India and China, they wanted to go there too. But the Muslim Empire lay between Europe and the East, so the European merchants were not able to get there by land – though a few, like *Marco Polo*, succeeded.

If they could not reach China by land, the Europeans thought, then perhaps they could get there by sea. This is one reason why they began developing better ships, and studying maps and navigation. It was then that the Greek and Arab theories about the earth being round came in useful. If the earth was flat, then of course it would be impossible to sail around it to China. But if it were *round!* Then that was a different matter.

By the late fifteenth century the small feudal kingdoms of the Middle Ages had developed into the strong nation states of England, France, Holland, Spain and Portugal. These nation states were very different from the feudal kingdoms from which they had evolved. They had strong central governments headed by a powerful king, backed by a strong army. Instead of clergy and landed knights, the most influential group in the country were the new middle class or bourgeoisie, whose power came from money rather than from inherited land or titles. This money which they earned through trade and commerce helped the kings equip and maintain strong armies which were able to defeat opposing groups of medieval knights. Moreover, since many more people now lived in towns, there was a much greater demand for goods of all kinds, luxuries, as well as the necessities such as food and household goods which rural people had traditionally been able to grow or make themselves.

Another characteristic of this new society was its questioning attitude toward old ideas. It was this intellectual curiosity that encouraged the new technology that we have read about. It was the same kind of curiosity that led people to wonder what might lie beyond lands already known. This curiosity added to the desire for increased trade and wealth, and led to a desire in Western Europe to find new routes to the fabled East. There might be found inexhaustible supplies of such luxuries as silks, spices, and, above all, gold which was the basis of all European currencies. Such discoveries would increase the wealth of the middle classes, and the glory and power of the kings. If only a new route to India and China could be found:

In 1492 Columbus set sail from Spain . . .

A Crusader. Notice that the crusader's armour is made from metal links. What do you think the advantages and disadvantages were of this sort of armour?

Things to do and think about

1 The Greeks thought that citizens *ought* to take part in politics. How do people in your country feel about citizens entering politics? Why do we not have 'direct democracy' today?

2 Compare the life of a European serf with that of an Inca commoner, and an Arawak.

3 Find out what you can about the mariner's compass and the *astrolabe*. Show how these helped seamen to navigate the oceans.

4 A great deal of time and money was spent on religious buildings and sculpture in the Middle Ages. Using the encyclopaedia, find out what you can about medieval art, and especially Gothic architecture. Compare European cathedrals with Aztec temples.

5 Find out what you can about Muhammad and the Muslim religion. Those of you who are Muslim can perhaps give a little talk to the class on the subject. Compare the difference between Christian and Islamic architecture by looking at pictures.

6 Towns in the Middle Ages were centres of progress. Is this also true of your country? Why do people migrate to towns?

7 We have seen that the Crusades helped stimulate progress in Europe. Do wars today still stimulate progress?

8 Why did the Europeans and not the Arabs, discover the New World?

9 By the fifteenth century, Europeans had developed a lot of new technology and they often looked down on the people they found whose technology was different to their own. Do you think this view was justified? Give reasons for your answer.

10 European explorers were not prepared for the advanced cultures they found in the New World. Do a project comparing European society in the fifteenth and sixteenth centuries with Amerindian societies in one (or several) of the following areas: Transportation and communication; Agriculture and land ownership; Government and law; Position of women; Architecture and building.

The first Europeans set out . . .

90

Finding what you need to know

Part One: The First To Come

By using the page references in this table you will
be able to compare the differences and similarities
between the five main groups of people who were
the first to inhabit the American continent.

	ARAWAK	AZTEC	CARIB	INCA	MAYA
Clothing	54	41	57	46	34
Communications	54	37	59	48	34
Food	13–14/54	40	56–57	45–46	34
Government	51–52	39	60	44–45	32–33
Housing	54–55	41	57	45	34
Leaders	51–52	37	57, 60	43–44	33
Legal system	51	39	59	48	32–33
Everyday life	53–54	39–42	56–57	45–47	34–35

Part Two: The Newcomers

Those who came later, the Africans, East Indians,
Chinese and Europeans, were widely scattered.

Because of their very different backgrounds,
similar comparisons would be of little value, but
the following list will help you to find particular
points about their origins and history.

Acknowledgements

The Publishers are grateful to the following for permission to reproduce photographs:–

American Museum of Natural History for page 13; Art Institute of Chicago for page 73; Bodleian Library, Oxford for page 21; British Museum for pages 66 and 89; Carnegie Institute of Washington for page 29; J Allan Cash for page 17, 27, 80 and 86; Cresset Press for page 81; Eldon Studies for page 25; Eliot Elisofen for page 67; Field Museum of Natural History for page 6; Museum of Fine Art, Boston for page 83; Museum Rietberg, Zurich for page 68; Photoresources for page 72; Picturepoint for page 77; Popperfoto for pages 65, 76 and 87; Thames and Hudson for pages 8, 30 and 33 from *Ancient Sun Kingdoms* by Victor Von Hagen.

Books from which illustrations have been adapted or upon which they have been based:

Bureau of American Ethnology, Handbook of South American Indians; S. Bleeker, The Eskimo, *Dobson, London*; R. Calder, The Inheritors, *Heinemann, London*; R. Carrington, The Dawn of History Series, The Early Days of Man, *Chatto and Windus, London*; H. E. Driver, Indians of North America, *University of Chicago Press*; B. Davidson and F. K. Buah, The Growth of African Civilisation, *Longmans, London*; M. C. English, An Outline of Nigerian History, *Longmans, London*; V. W. von Hagen, Ancient Sun Kingdoms of the Americas, *Thames and Hudson, London*; The Incas, People of the Sun, *Brockhampton Press, Leicester*; World of the Maya, *World Publishing Company, New York*; Aztec, Man and Tribe, *New American Library, New York*; T. A. Joyce, Central American and West Indian Archaeology, *Macmillan and Philip Lee, London*; P. R. Kirby, The Musical Instruments of the Native Races of South Africa, *Oxford University Press, London*; R. S. Rattray, Religion and Art in Ashanti, *Clarendon Press, Oxford*.